A Gift For

_____

From

_____

Catch
of the Day

SPIRITUAL LESSONS FOR LIFE
FROM THE SPORT OF FISHING

JIMMY HOUSTON

COUNTRYMAN

NASHVILLE, TENNESSEE

Project Editor: Kathy Baker

Designed by The DesignWorks Group, Sisters, Oregon;
        Cover, David Uttley; interior, Robin Black
        www.thedesignworksgroup.com

ISBN 1–4041–0194–2

Printed and bound in Belgium

www.jcountryman.com | www.thomasnelson.com

January

GENESIS 1:1

In the beginning God created the sky and the earth.

IT'S ALWAYS EXCITING to begin something new like a new job, new house, new marriage, or a new baby. New projects excite and energize me. I'm always excited about beginning a new tournament season where all the fishermen start out again at zero. I can't wait for the start of major league baseball or the first game of Oklahoma University football or basketball.

One tradition I started more than thirty years ago was to begin each January 1 and read the Bible through in a year. Now, I've completely read the Bible through more than thirty times in addition to my other Bible reading and study. Start your very own tradition today. Five, ten, twenty years from now, you'll be amazed at what God wants to tell you on a daily basis.

tip

Use the cold winter months to clean and organize all your tackle to get ready for that great spring fishin'.

GENESIS 1:27

So God created human beings in his image.

GOD COULD HAVE MADE US look like anything
He wanted. We could have looked like the space
aliens we see on *Star Trek* or *Men in Black*.
We could have looked like frogs or fish or anything
else God chose. But He chose to pattern us after
Himself. We are patterned after God—physically,
emotionally, and spiritually. We are
not God, we are not perfect, but we
are patterned to be that way.

   The next time you have a
pity party about how you look or
feel, think about what God
could have made you look like
and how He could have made
you feel. Look in that mirror and
smile. Look in yourself and laugh;
God patterned you and me after
Himself!

tip

Spool on new line
at the start of every year
and every 4 to 6 weeks
during fishin' season.

JANUARY 3

PROVERBS 10:2

Riches gotten by doing wrong have no value, but right living will save you from death.

FISHING TOURNAMENTS have brought out the very best and very worst in fishermen. While tournaments are incredibly fair and honest, cheating does creep in sometimes. Blatant cheating is usually discovered quickly and cheaters are disqualified, generally banned for life. Unintentional rule–breaking is punished by penalties such as a weight penalty or loss of your catch for that day. The most damaging cheaters are the ones who bend the rules for their own benefit and ill–gotten gain. These anglers are bending or breaking the rules with almost no chance of ever being caught. Those gains will never last. Opportunities for ill–gotten gain come into our lives all the time. While we may never be caught, our very life may depend on how we handle these temptations to cheat!

†ip

Bass are not very aggressive in cold water. Use slow moving baits and be patient.

JANUARY 4

LUKE 12:34

"Your heart will be where your treasure is."

EVERY FISHERMAN has their favorite bait. For me it's a Terminator spinnerbait for bass and a Road Runner for crappie. Single baits, but within each bait category is a wide variety of colors, sizes and even different types of materials. We treasure these baits because we can have success in just about every situation.

If our treasure is Jesus, we have a God we can rely on in all of life's situations. If our thoughts are on Jesus, we become a better friend, co–worker, husband, or wife. We also become a more likeable, friendlier person even to strangers!

tip

Slow rolling a white spinnerbait with a large Oklahoma blade works great for lethargic wintertime bass.

PSALM 31:24

All you who put your hope in the LORD be strong and brave.

BETTER FISHERMEN DO NOT HOPE for success or rely on luck in order to catch fish. They pin their hopes on facts, skills, knowledge, and experience. The more of these we have, the more fish we catch and the more consistent we become. Similarly, the more we know and experience about Jesus, the better we will be at becoming the kind of person we want to be and who God wants us to be. This doesn't happen overnight. It takes time to become a great fisherman, so be strong; it also takes time for God to mold us into the person we will become. The great part is that God allows us the opportunity to become better every day we stay close to Him!

†ip

Pork trailers on jigs and spinnerbaits work better than soft plastics in cold water.

MATTHEW 28:20

"*. . . and I will be with you always , even until the end of this age.*"

FISHING IS A SPORT most enjoyed with someone else. Sure, we can fish alone and have fun, but it is always more enjoyable with a friend or another member of your family. My closest fishin' partner is my wife, Chris. My most memorable days fishin' are not great tournament victories but days spent with her or fishin' with my kids or grandkids.

† i p

Vertical jig your Road Runners during the winter months to catch more crappie.

God never intended for us to be alone. That's why He sent Jesus. That is why when we are saved, God places His Holy Spirit in us. No matter how isolated or alone we may feel at times, Jesus is always there. All we need to do is call on Him.

PROVERBS 10:22

*The LORD's blessing brings wealth and no sorrow comes
with it.*

THE OTHER DAY, I asked a guy in another boat,
"I wonder what the poor people are doing today?"
He answered "They're fishing."

Fishing is one of those blessings from God
that makes us rich, no matter what our bank
account says. Too often though, we dwell on the
sorrows the devil throws at us rather than the
blessings we have. This is exactly what the devil
wants; he's working to ruin our day and our life.
As a Christian and a child of God, we cannot
accept that. Today, write down ten or fifteen of the
blessings God has laid on your life.
Before you get half done, the devil
will be hard pressed having a chance
to ruin your day. By the way,
this little trick will work again
tomorrow.

†ip

Lighter line is
more manageable in
cold conditions and will
get you more bites.

PSALM 86:5

Lord, you are kind and forgiving and have great love
for those who call to you.

FISHERMEN SINCE THE BEGINNING of time have
been asking for help and advice on how to catch
more fish. Jesus told Peter where to cast his net,
and some of us today make our living telling others
how to become better fishermen. I know people
who have driven hundreds of miles to listen to a
top tournament pro give a seminar. They do this
just to be more successful on the water.

God is the ultimate expert, and He
is ready and willing to answer our
questions and to come to our aid.
All we need to do is to ask. But
somehow—out of "macho–ness",
lack of faith, or whatever—we'll
not come to God and ask until
it's the last resort. If we'll get God
involved in today's problems and
concerns right now, we'll likely not
need to use God as the last resort
tomorrow.

†ip

Standing treetops
often hold bass
in clear water lakes
throughout the
winter months.

2 TIMOTHY 3:16

All scripture is given by God and is useful for teaching,
for showing people what is wrong in their lives,
for correcting faults, and for teaching how to live right.

WE'RE ALLOWED THREE DAYS to practice for a
BASS (Bass Anglers Sportsman Society)
tournament. Most competitors will tell you this is
the time to locate the fish and figure out what lures
and tactics will work best in order to have success
during the actual competition. Just as important,
however, is learning the places where you cannot
catch fish and what baits won't work!

When God's word is read (the Bible) and
spoken (preached), it lays out what God will
do for us. It also directly focuses on
problem areas in our lives! Open the
Bible anywhere and start reading,
God will soon tell you about
changes you need to make to
improve your life, and then He'll
help you make those changes.
God loves us so much, He wants
to make us better every day.

†ip

Slightly open up
the hook on your
spinnerbait for better
hookups and fewer
missed bass!

PSALM 14:2

The LORD looked down from heaven on all people . . .

WE WEAR POLARIZED SUNGLASSES when fishing in order to be able to see down into the water. Polarization removes the glare from the surface and allows us to see a foot or two or even more into clear water. This is helpful. We can see stumps, rocks, logs, and other hiding places for the fish. We sometimes can even see the fish!

†ip

Remember to visit a heated fishing dock for a very comfortable wintertime crappie outing.

It's pretty awesome that God can see us all and yet focus on each of us individually. How would we treat our family, friends, or even perfect strangers if we knew God was there looking over our shoulders? Well, He is! Keep this in mind today when someone messes up your order at the drive–through, disappoints you, or cuts you off in traffic. Live today trying to impress God . . . you just might do it!

2 THESSALONIANS 1:11

That is why we pray for you, asking our God to help you live the kind of life he called you to live.

COMPETITION BREEDS PRAYER. I believe almost all tournament fishermen pray, even the non–Christians. Most of the time, when we pray, we're praying for His glory. We're asking God to do something special, something supernatural for us. Today, direct your prayers into praying for someone else. Lift up your family, friends, pastor, and co–workers. Pray for that person at the drive–up window and even your enemies or someone who has done you wrong. It's pretty difficult for me to pray for someone who has wronged me, but when I do, God creates some peace in my heart where before there was pain. Dedicate your prayers today to others, and your God will receive the glory.

† i p

Steeper banks will
produce more fish
during the
cold winter months.

EXODUS 20:3

You must not have any other gods except me.

FOR MANY PEOPLE, their passion about something becomes their religion.

Fishing is one of those passions that can become almost a religious experience. I don't know how many times I've heard someone talk about getting close to God on the lake. Others tell me they can worship God better on the lake Sunday than in church with a bunch of Christians who might be hypocrites. But when we do this, we're not worshiping God at all. We're making fishing our god. At the very least, we're guilty of worshiping God's creation. This is really the same as worshiping the moon or the stars. God commands us to assemble to worship Him and Him only!

†ip
A shad die-off in extremely cold weather will trigger good bass fishing.

JANUARY 13

JAMES 1:12

When people are tempted and still continue strong,
they should be happy. After they have proved their faith,
God will reward them with life forever.

"WHY ME, LORD?" How many times have we all
uttered these words in times of struggle or testing?
I wonder sometimes on the lake how many things
can go wrong. "If this is a test, Lord,
I'd rather take a written one!" Either
we can react to these trials with
frustration, anger, and even foul
language or we can react with
patience. God promises to bless
us when we patiently endure.
A day fishing is seldom perfect,
just like a day doing anything
else is seldom perfect. How we
handle these breakdowns, or tests, is
what is important. We can be patient
and be blessed or we can blow it—and what does
that really accomplish anyway?

tip

Check the diameter
of your fishing line.
Different lines have
different diameters, even in
the same-pound tests.

PSALM 33:7

He gathered the water of the sea into a heap.
He made the great ocean stay in its place.

LAKESIDE VIEWS. Desktop fountains. Backyard
ponds. Water captivates us all, and it is, of course,
even more important to fishermen. We really can't
help but have a love affair with water, but do we
have that same fascination and love for the awesome
God who created and controls that water? When I
look at a lake, river, or stream, I'm always reminded
how much God loves us to create something we
enjoy so much. I also realize that God has set
boundaries on how we are to live our lives.
Those boundaries are for our own good.
Living within God's boundaries not
only pleases Him, it keeps us out of all
sorts of calamities and sin.

tip

Seek out the
clearer water areas
when water temperatures
are low.

ANUARY 15

MARK 2:10

"But I will prove to you that the Son of Man has authority on earth to forgive sins."

TALK IS BIG sometimes during practice rounds at bass tournaments. Even when fishermen fail to catch much on tournament day, they still brag about all the big ones they caught in practice. The real proof is carrying those bass to the weigh–in scales.

Jesus claimed authority to forgive sins. He backed this up by making the blind see, the lame walk, and the dead come back to life. He ultimately backed this up by His death on the cross and resurrection three days later. He then walked among the living here on earth for forty more days. Jesus can and will forgive our sins if we ask Him. He will also carry us to that great weigh–in in Heaven!

†ip

Fish where muddy water and clear water are mixing together.

MARK 4:25

"Those who have understanding will be given more."

WITHOUT A DOUBT, knowledge and understanding
are the keys to becoming a better fisherman.
The fisherman who "knows it all" will very
seldom develop into a consistent fish–catcher.
Those who are open to instruction and criticism
will become champions.

We open up to God's teaching by praying
consistently and then by acting upon the ways
God answers those prayers. If we're consistent
in acting within what God says to do,
we'll gain more understanding about
Him and His direction for our
lives. This direction will become
evident to our family and friends,
and it will even be seen by folks
we don't know. Develop a daily,
consistent prayer life, and your
relationship with God and your
understanding of God will grow on a
daily basis.

+ i p

Fish always
face into the current.
Cast your bait upstream
and let it flow
into the
fish's position.

JANUARY 17

PSALM 37:3

Trust the LORD and do good.

I FINISHED THIRD in a BASS tournament on Lake Powell, Arizona. Fred Ward won, Larry Nixon was second, and we were all fishing 113 miles or so from takeoff and weigh–in. To travel 113 miles, one way, was putting a tremendous amount of trust in that big Mercury outboard. By placing trust in that motor, I did well. We all did well and we prospered.

No matter what, we can't fail when we place our trust in the God who created us. We're not always going to prosper in everything we do. We will falter at times, but I know this: I have victory and safety and prosperity in Jesus regardless of what might go wrong today. This trust in Him will carry me safely through.

†ip

After a cold front, try a white marabou Road Runner with a fluorescent red head.

MATTHEW 13:41

"The Son of Man will send out his angels,
and they will gather out of his kingdom all
who cause sin and all who do evil."

RAY SCOTT, the founder of the Bass Anglers
Sportsman Society, has a great belief that
angels have been a big part of his life
and have played a major part in the
startup and growth of BASS.
He believes God has sent humans
as angels to assist him in times
of need.

†ip

Use translucent
soft plastics in clear water.
You can almost
see through them.

The Bible teaches of angels
and promises that God will
provide angels for the protection of
His people. He will also use angels to
do away with all the causes of sin. There will
come a time when everything on earth will be
made perfect. There will be no need for news
reports that dwell on earth's problems, because
there will be no problems. This is the Good News
of all who have Jesus Christ as their personal Savior.

JANUARY 19

PSALM 18:1

I love you, LORD. You are my strength.

TOURNAMENT BASS FISHING is a much more physical sport than most non–tournament fishermen realize. Most of us do not carry a front seat in our boat, so we have to stand constantly while fishing. I also do not eat or drink anything during competition hours. Tournaments also usually allow very little time for sleep. You need strength to endure.

Whether or not you are a believer, your strength in every aspect of life comes from God. He has divinely made us to do almost miraculous things. No machine, robot, or even that Energizer bunny can keep going like we can. Today, pay special attention to the physical abilities God has given you to just keep going and going. Thank Him for this and give Him your praise and love.

tip

Spray Reel Magic on your reels two or three times every day to give you more casting distance.

EXODUS 18:20

"Warn them about the laws and teachings, and teach
them the right way to live and what they should do."

FISHING IS A SPORT where our results are
determined by the decisions we make. Every
day on the water we make hundreds of
decisions. Sometimes we might have to
choose among only two or three
options, while other times we might
have to select among two hundred
or three hundred possibilities. Very
seldom will we make the very best
decision each time in a day, and
the trick is to make decisions that
are more on the better side than on
the worse side. These are our decisions.

†ip

Fish directly below
dams and spillways
for great white bass, striper,
and catfish action.

We are told to conduct our lives based on
God's decisions, laws, and instruction. Why should
we do this? Because God's decisions will produce
the very best results in our lives. This is true for all
aspects of life, including our families, our jobs, our
spare time, even our eating habits. God truly does
know what is best for us!

JANUARY 21

LUKE 8:38

*"Go back home and tell people how much
God has done for you."*

SOME FISHING PATTERNS are like the seasons;
they are only productive during a short time.
For example, the spawn only last a few weeks,
so fishing bedding fish is a short-term opportunity.
The time that fish actively school is usually just a
short period each year. Certain lures are super-
effective only a few weeks each year.

Jesus spent a mere thirty-three years on earth
about two thousand years ago. He repeatedly told
those He encountered to tell others about their
experiences with Him. He wanted to make sure we
knew who He was, why He came, and especially
how much He loves us, our friends,
and our families.

This Jesus, our Savior, the one
we trust and depend on to get us to
Heaven and eternal life, is now
depending on us to tell others how
much He has done for you and
me. Be sure to tell someone today.

†ip

A 10-inch or
11-inch worm works well
in lakes with lots
of grass.

PROVERBS 25:28

Those who do not control themselves are like a city whose walls are broken down.

FISHING A SPINNERBAIT is all about control. The best spinnerbait fisherman is the one who can control the bait. This begins with great casting accuracy, but it also includes retrieval speed, depth, and even angles of presentation.

Controlling our temper, words, thoughts, and actions on a daily basis can be a real challenge. When we lose our self–control, we say and do things we later regret. Not to mention it drives our blood pressure sky high. The easiest way to maintain self–control is to live each day as close to God as we can. I try to do this by praying a lot, thanking and praising God in my prayers. Listening to praise and gospel music also helps. If we are concentrating on our God, then we'll have less trouble controlling our self.

tip

Use a coffee cup or coffee can to practice your casting on days when you can't go fishin'.

JANUARY 23

JAMES 3:8

. . . but no one can tame the tongue.

THE MOST IDENTIFIABLE WAY to tell the difference between a largemouth bass and a spotted bass is the tongue. Spotted bass have a patch of teeth on their tongue. When you rub your finger over the tongue, the teeth are very easy to feel.

It seems that most of us have fangs on our tongues at times. The bad thing is once we have said something, we can't take it back. Perhaps just as evil as speaking something bad *to* someone is saying bad things *about* someone.

The devil uses gossip to destroy relationships. He makes it fun to spread a little dirt and exaggerate the facts. I pray every day to have God keep me from saying anything bad about anyone. I fail often, but God isn't finished with me.

tip

Fish prefer rocky banks in the winter because the rocks give more heat.

JANUARY 24

PHILIPPIANS 4:8

*Brothers and sisters, think about the things
that are good and worthy of praise.
Think about the things that are true and honorable
and right and pure and beautiful and respected.*

BASS TOURNAMENT FISHERMEN are some of the
most focused of all competitors. We must
concentrate for long periods of time, and if we lose
that concentration even for just a cast or two, it can
cost us dearly.

As men and women of God, we are
instructed to concentrate on all the good
things God puts in our lives. Why? If we
concentrate on these, we'll most likely act upon
these thoughts. We will be treating others
the way God intends us to treat them.
If our thoughts are dishonorable and
evil instead, we are apt to act on
these thoughts in our relationships.
Of course, this does not please
God but pleases the devil instead.
Think of something pure,
honorable or lovely . . . right now!

†ip

Ponds warm up
2–3 weeks earlier than
large reservoirs,
making for great
early season fishing.

JANUARY 25

2 TIMOTHY 1:12

. . . .but I am not ashamed, because I know Jesus, the One in whom I have believed. And I am sure he is able to protect what he has trusted me with until that day.

FISHERMEN RELY ON information from others to help us plan our fishin' trips. We look at lake levels and conditions, read fishing reports, and even call our friends to find out where the fish are biting and what they are biting on.

As a born–again Christian, all the information I need in life, God has put in His word, the Bible, and the greatest friend I have is Jesus Christ. While fishing information may be sketchy, outdated or just downright wrong, God's information never changes and never has errors. God's word promises that Jesus will return. I have entrusted to Him my very soul, and most importantly I've entrusted it to Him for eternity.

†ip

Live bait often
will catch fish
in cold weather when
artificial fail.

PROVERBS 27:9

The sweet smell of perfume and oils is pleasant,
and so is good advice from a friend.

TOURNAMENT ANGLERS SELDOM GO it alone
during competition. Most have one or two close
friends to confide in as they try to solve the
mysteries of how to succeed on any given lake.
We trust that our friends want our success just as
much as their own.

In the same way, a Christian's main source of
counsel should be pastors, deacons, and the rest of
the church family. This is one of the very great
benefits of belonging to, attending, and working in
God's church. Many individuals who claim
Christianity and claim Jesus as their
Lord and Savior do not participate in a
local church, but according to
God's word, this is not what He
intended. God built His church
for His people to be involved in
for their mutual benefit and for
His glory.

tip
Mid to late
afternoons are
better for
winter fishin'.

PSALM 108:13

. . . but we can win with God's help.

EGO IS A GREAT stumbling block for most of us.
It can hurt us in our attempts to catch fish or can
impede just about anything else we try to
accomplish. That ego inside of us just presses on to
make us want to do it all on our own. That's not
God's way. He wants to help; in fact, He even
insists on helping. The children of Israel succeeded
at every turn when they depended on God's help,
but they failed miserably when they acted on their
own without God's help. Even with these examples,
we try to do things our way and call on God only
when our way fails. Why not call on God first?

What does God want to help with?
Everything. From the smallest part of
our lives to the most important.

† ι ρ

Customize your
lures by adding
a little red to them.

JANUARY 28

JAMES 4:7

So give yourselves completely to God. Stand against the devil, and the devil will run from you.

I'VE SEEN SOME TOURNAMENT **competitors** become downright obnoxious when they were doing well and placing high or winning. Tournament fishing, however, has a way of humbling everyone, no matter who you are or how much you've won.

God loves humility and the devil hates it. God hates arrogance and the devil loves it, and he will spend a great deal of time on us trying to convince us how great we are, what a great thing we did, or how much we have accomplished. Not only is such pride a sin, it undoubtedly will carry a price tag with it. Jesus humbled Himself to the point of dying on the cross. He washed the feet of His disciples and lowered Himself to the position of servant at every opportunity. What a great example to you and me!

†ip
Going to the upper ends of creeks and rivers is the easiest way to locate fish on strange lakes.

Catch of the Day   31

PSALM 119:30

I have chosen the way of truth; I have obeyed your laws.

ONE OF THE MOST DIFFICULT things for me in fishing and hunting is to know the laws in each state I am in. I once got a citation after a show aired on television. We were catfishing with Yo–Bobs, which are kind of like jug lining. Kansas law requires these to be anchored to the bottom of the lake. I had called the local game ranger and asked him what the laws were, but he either didn't know or failed to mention this anchoring part. His boss, who saw the show, knew the law, and both the ranger and I were in trouble.

God's laws are simple yet straightforward. He tells us these laws in His word and He actually writes these laws on our hearts. He does this because His laws are for our benefit. What an awesome God!

†ip
A five–foot ultralight rod will make even the smallest of fish fun to catch.

JEREMIAH 31:33

*"I will put my teachings in their minds
and write them on their hearts."*

SOME PEOPLE JUST SEEM to be born with the
ability to catch fish. I've often said that Chris
(my wife), Roland Martin, and Larry Nixon
were the most natural-born anglers I
have ever fished with. They all have
an amazing God-given talent to
figure out how to catch fish. Sure,
they have great skills, but they
also have that extra sense about
fishing that most other anglers—
including me—don't possess.
God has promised to place in us
this extraordinary sense to know in our
minds and feel in our hearts exactly what we
need to do and think to please Him. All we must
do is follow and obey. The result will be the great
blessings God has promised. I fail often, but
praise God He has written these laws with a
permanent marker!

†ip
Evergreen trees
make excellent structure
to place in your
favorite fishin' hole.

EPHESIANS 4:29

When you talk, do not say harmful things, but say what people need—words that will help others become stronger.

BOB FERRIS WAS THE BEST bass tournament announcer of all time. He announced Bass'n Gal tournaments for all twenty–one years of the organization. Yes, he had a big, booming voice and tremendous stage presence, but what made him great was what he said and the way he said it. He made all the girls feel important and always encouraged them just enough to make them believe they had a great chance to catch fish and do well in the tournaments.

In daily life, if each of us went about trying to be helpful and encourage those with whom we come in contact, the whole world would be a better place to live. Not only that, we would be encouraged and helped by those around us.

tip

Always wet your knots before cinching them down.

February

PSALM 90:12
*Teach us how short our lives really
are so that we may be wise.*

TOURNAMENT FISHING IS not only an effort to
catch bass; it's a monumental struggle against time.
Perhaps our most important use of time is the
three days we have to practice for a tournament.
If we use that time wisely, we'll probably have a
great tournament. God says that using our time
well will grow our wisdom. I believe that God
wants us going about doing things that are
important to Him. Some of our time every day
must be spent praying (talking to God). Some
must be spent in God's word (God talking
to us). Some of our time must
be used to tell others what Jesus
is doing in our lives (talking about
God). I know I need to grow in
wisdom and am thankful God has
a plan for me to do just that.

tip

Always make sure
your crankbait
or jerkbait is running
perfectly straight.

PROVERBS 13:21

Trouble always comes to sinners,
but good people enjoy success.

SOME DAYS WE FEEL LIKE we are walking under a
cloud that rains only on us. Our boat won't start,
the fish won't bite, we break a rod, and so forth.
One trouble simply leads to another. Sometimes
much of life seems just like that. Mostly we blame
others or other situations, but God
tells us our sins may be creating our
problems. If trouble chases sinners,
then trouble will catch up most of
the time, if not all the time.
That's the bad news. The good
news is that God is ready,
willing, and able to forgive
these sins. When we repent of
these sins and ask God's
forgiveness, He erases our wrongness
and replaces it with the righteousness of
Jesus. What chases us then is the abundance of
God's blessings.

tip
Blue and red
are the basic colors
that bass can
see best.

LUKE 21:19

"By continuing to have faith you will save your lives."

JESUS TOLD THOSE WORDS to His disciples after warning them that they would be persecuted for their allegiance to Him. This verse helped strengthen me as I was chastised for refusing to wear a beer patch on my tournament shirt or place a beer brand decal on my boat. Not only was I criticized by non–Christians, but by Christian fishermen as well. My stand against promoting or selling alcohol is a long–standing one. We own a big convenience and tackle store on Lake Tenkiller, Oklahoma, where we have never sold beer. I'm told that this position costs me $40,000 per year in profit.

Jesus told us to stand firm. We can't put a price tag on what we believe, and Jesus has already paid the price for our souls. So . . . stand firm.

†í ρ
Use backing when filling your casting reels with new line. This will save you money and time.

JOSHUA 24:15

"As for me and my family, we will serve the Lord."

CHOICES ABOUND IN FISHING. From the moment
we even start to think about going fishing, we start
making choices. Making those choices is part of the
fun in fishing, and the better the choices the better
the fishing and the fishing trip.

We have only one choice to make about
Jesus: we believe in Him or we don't.
Our choice not only makes a tremendous
difference in our trip through this life, but
it makes a difference for eternity. That
difference: heaven or hell! Whom will you
serve today? What about your family? We
have so many choices today, but any
choice other than serving the Lord
will end in complete failure.

†ip
Willow leaf blades
produce better
in clear water.

FEBRUARY 5

PROVERBS 1:18

But sinners will fall into their own traps;
they will only catch themselves!

NO ONE LIKES TO BE TOLD they've messed up, made a mistake, or failed. Over the years, ESPN has told us what they see wrong in our televised fishing shows. We can't ignore that criticism, so we accept it and work double hard to make the show better, even if we believe we're right and they are wrong. The result is generally a better show.

The next time someone criticizes you, use it to your advantage. According to God's word, the trick is to accept it. Don't ignore it, don't make excuses, don't argue about it. Accept the criticism and look for a positive way to build upon it. That will bring success and honor.

tip

The colder the water, the slower you need to work your lures.

PSALM 112:5

It is good to be merciful and generous.

LURES CAN GET PRETTY EXPENSIVE on the water.
I've told many a partner I've got one more lure just
like the one I'm catching fish on but it will really
cost them. Seriously, almost any fisherman will give
a hot lure to his partner. At a BASS tournament
this year on Lake Guntersville, Alabama, I gave my
partner the jerkbait, rod, reel, line, and everything
I had just caught my limit on. He could not
believe it, but I wanted him to catch fish. God
expects and intends for us to be generous not only
with our money, but also our time. When we give
of ourselves and our resources we will
always receive much more in return.
That return might not be immediate,
but it will definitely come about in
God's good time.

+ i p

Check your
rod tips and guides
periodically for breaks
or cracks that
can damage your line.

PROVERBS 19:21

People can make all kinds of plans,
but only the LORD's plan will happen.

WHEN WE STARTED the Bible study at the
tournaments back in 1983, I had no idea what God
had in store. This Bible study group quickly turned
into FOCAS, the Fellowship of Christian Anglers
Society. Today, FOCAS has more than eight
thousand members and more than 125 chapters
scattered around the world, including Africa. We
still have FOCAS Bible studies even to this day.

All I knew was that I was missing a lot of
church during fishing tournaments, while I still
needed fellowship with other Christians. God's
purpose was much larger . . . saving
lost souls and changing lives! Praise
God that I followed His leadership
with my plans. Whatever you do
today, include God in all of your
plans. He has a purpose for
everything you do, and His
purpose is not only the best . . .
it will prevail!

†ίρ

Develop a
simple game plan
for each
day's tournament.

ROMANS 7:6

So now we serve God in a new way with the Spirit,
and not in the old way with written rules.

FISHING HAS CHANGED so much over the last
several years. Most of the hot lures today were not
even around as few as three or four years ago. All of
our equipment is so much better. These new ways
to fish have certainly made the game better.

Jesus has brought about the new way to serve
God. He has re-explained the law and put
His Spirit and commandments in our hearts.
We worship out of thanks and praise
for what Jesus has done for each of
us. Worship Him today by
demonstrating His love to
everyone you meet. Praise Him
by letting His Spirit guide
you in every situation you're
involved in. Now, let's serve
God in all we do.

†ip

Early season
sport shows are
a great place to learn
more about fishing.
Attend every seminar.

1 CORINTHIANS 10:13

The only temptation that has come to you is that which everyone has. But you can trust God, who will not permit you to be tempted more than you can stand.

EVEN THE MOST HONEST of all tournament fishermen will still have situations come up that will allow them to bend the rules. These are temptations, and I believe they come from the devil. We're told that everyone is attacked by these temptations, but as children of God we always have a way out. That way out can come in many forms, but I believe the easiest way out is simple prayer.

No matter how attractive the devil makes temptations look, don't forget or neglect to pray your way out.

Ask God to show you the way, and according to His promise, He will.

†ip

Tip your Road Runner with a live minnow when fishing is extremely tough.

ACTS 13:38

*But through Jesus everyone who believes
is free from all sins.*

ONE YEAR, MY WIFE, Chris, won so much
during the Bass'n Gal tournaments she actually
began to feel guilty about winning. I really
believe she lost the Bass'n Gal Classic
that year because of those guilt
feelings. She claims that's not
true.
Of course we shouldn't feel
guilty about winning.

We carry a huge burden of
guilt for the sinful things we do in
our lives. This burden can affect all
aspects of our daily lives. Belief in Jesus
will free us of that guilt. This is what God's
gospel is about, removing the guilt and declaring us
right with almighty God. This gives you and me
the freedom to make the most out of every day
God gives us free from guilt, free from sin, and
right with God.

tip

Fish close
to the shoreline
when fishing ponds
(or tanks as they are
called in Texas).

FEBRUARY 11

PSALM 91:11

He has put his angels in charge of you to watch over you
wherever you go.

OVER THE YEARS, I've had many close calls on the
water. One came when I was 16 years old baiting a
trotline at night in February. I was with my good
friend Bobby Ballew, and the water was icy cold.
Our boat capsized with only the nose remaining
above the water. We had just enough room to put
one finger each in the bow eye and hold on and
yell for help. Our one light shined on the
mountainside across the lake and
hypothermia was setting in.
Miraculously, someone in a
house heard us and rescued us
in a small boat. We had been
in the icy waters for longer
than forty minutes! Too long
to still be alive, but we were.
That's my God!

tip

Smashing your barbs down
on a Road Runner will
allow you to get unsnagged
easier, thus reducing the
number of lures
you lose.

PROVERBS 15:15

Every day is hard for those who suffer,
but a happy heart is like a continual feast.

SOME FISHERMEN SEEM to be happy all the time
no matter what. They seem to be having a good
time and smiling under all circumstances. Is it
possible that some people never have problems? Of
course not. We all experience problems,
and God says every day brings trouble for
some people. For the poor, this can be
just having enough to eat, but for
those who belong to God, life will
still be abundant. Most of us have
never had to worry about having
enough to eat, but we still will
have many days filled with
trouble. Making sure we have real
happiness in our hearts will
overcome all our problems. When we
realize what Jesus did for us, how much He
loves us, and what He has prepared for us . . .
it should be easy to have a happy heart.

† i p

Bass will move to
points near outside bends
in creek channels
in early spring.

HEBREWS 10:24

Let us think about each other and help each other
to show love and do good deeds.

TOURNAMENT FISHERMEN WEAR their names on
their shirts. This makes it easy for fishing fans to
know who's who at tournaments. Without nametags
it would be tough. Even extremely recognized
anglers can be confusing. For instance, folks often
mistake Roland Martin and me for each other.
I've always thought the whole world would get
along better if everyone wore a nametag.
Just simply calling someone by their first name
is encouragement.

Spend today trying to build up those
you encounter. Use every
opportunity to say something
nice about everyone you talk to.
It won't be long until your
encouragement spurs others into
doing and saying positive things
to and about others. With just a
little effort, you're spreading love.

tip

Use wide-wobbling
crank bait
in cold water.

PROVERBS 20:27

*The LORD looks deep inside people and
searches through their thoughts.*

I LOVE TO BASS FISH at night. Even on the
darkest of nights you can catch fish. I like to search
out boats docks that have mercury or vapor lights
on them. The added light helps casting
accuracy, but the light also attracts bugs,
which attract baitfish, which attracts
bass. One thing leads to another.

God not only knows and sees
everything we do, He also looks
within our spirits. What does this
mean? I believe it means God is
well aware of our heart and our
intentions even when we may be
able to fool everyone else. We are
laid bare before our almighty God.
He knows what in our hearts will lead
to which results. With this in mind,
I constantly ask God to create in me a pure heart
and spirit. I know that only God can make me the
way He wants me to be.

†ip

Use a red blade
on your spinnerbait
at night.

JEREMIAH 17:7

"But the person who trusts in the LORD will be blessed."

I'VE SAID MANY TIMES that if I'm not going to catch any fish, I'd rather not catch them on a spinnerbait. We all have our "confidence" baits and lures we trust to produce even when all else fails.

Jesus is my confidence in life. I wouldn't even try to live my life without Him. I can't see why anyone would try to raise a family, grow a marriage, or build a career without a close working relationship with Jesus. Life is just too difficult to go it alone. If you have something really pressing in your life, spend a little time in God's word and a little time talking with God. He has some remarkable solutions to whatever problems you have. He's also just waiting to help.

tip

Use an empty parking lot to learn how to back a boat trailer.

JOHN 15:15

*"But I call you friends, because I have made known
to you everything I heard from my Father."*

SOME OF MY MOST EXCITING days as a kid were
going fishing with my dad. We fished for
everything—crappie, catfish, white bass, and
largemouth bass. Much of what I learned about
fishing came from my father.

Much of the way I live my life is by what my
Father has told me in His word and by His
Holy Spirit. The decisions I make, the way I
try to treat others, and even my attitude are
determined by my heavenly Father. Folks
spend millions in our society trying to learn
how to improve themselves, look better,
be healthier, or make more money.
The list could almost go on forever.
The answers are really easy; Jesus
has already told us everything.

✝ip

Use a trailer hook
100% of the time
on spinnerbaits in
order to learn
how to use them.

ROMANS 15:13

Then your hope will overflow
by the power of the Holy Spirit.

FISHING IS MOST CERTAINLY a game of hope.
For most of us, including me, we just hope we get
to go fishing soon. Once we get on the water, we
have an abundance of hope resting on every cast.
Without hope we might as well
stay home.

Without God we have no hope
for eternity. God has instilled in
men the knowledge and desire
for eternal life. He has also
provided us with the way to
eternal life with Him. This way
is Jesus. Jesus died for our sins so
we could have eternal life with
Him in heaven. This is a Christian's
hope, and life would be meaningless
without it. Our life would simply be living
day–by–day fearing death. With Jesus, we are
assured of eternal life with God.

tip
Always carry
Dip-n-Dye or marker
pens to add color
to your lures.

NEHEMIAH 8:10

"Don't be sad, because the joy of the Lord
will make you strong."

MY WIFE, CHRIS, has always said that the great
thing about fishing is you don't have to be strong
or tall or fast or especially gifted to fish. I have
fished with many people who have significant
physical handicaps. We still had a lot of fun and
caught fish.

Nehemiah told the people the joy of the
Lord—not their physical abilities—was their
strength. Knowing Jesus on a personal basis
produces a joy that overcomes anything this world
can throw at us. It allows us to be strong no
matter how serious or how dejected we
might otherwise become. This joy is
difficult for a non–Christian to
understand, but it overflows in
one who knows Jesus.

tip

Have your
outboard tuned
in early spring
to save gas money
every fishing trip.

PROVERBS 3:9

Honor the LORD with your wealth
and the first fruits from all your crops.

DARREL ROBERTSON from Oklahoma won the first really giant purse in bass fishing . . . over $600,000 in the Ranger Millennium Tournament in 1999. Still today, this is one of the top biggest payouts ever. Darrel used $100,000 of that money to build a new activity center for his church. To a real believer, giving to the Lord is not an option; it's an honor. Tithes and offerings are not something you do if you can afford it. Tithes and offerings are something you do *before* you spend the rest of your money.

I believe if we do not tithe, we don't allow God to pour out His blessing on us. We actually cheat ourselves out of something God intended us to have.

tip
Throw at
any movement on
top the water.

JOHN 16:33

"In this world you will have trouble,
but be brave! I have defeated the world."

HOW WE HANDLE ADVERSITY is one of the great
traits of a champion fisherman. No matter how
good you get, how much knowledge, how great
your ability . . . trials will come, and they generally
will come often. This world is going to throw more
problems at us at times than we think we can bear.
This is because Satan is ruler of this world, and
that's the business Satan is about—causing
problems for everyone and especially
believers in Jesus. Can a Christian
handle adversity better than a
non–believer? Absolutely!

We live by faith that Jesus
has overcome the world and that
He is able to see us through
whatever Satan puts on our plate.
We never have to face these
tribulations alone.

TIP

Drag your
fishing line without
a lure behind the boat
to remove line twist.

PSALM 35:9

Then I will rejoice in the LORD;
I will be happy when he saves me.

MANY TOURNAMENT WINNERS today stand on the stage and thank God for their victories. Some even give Jesus the credit and glory for the win. I believe winning does indeed give a Christian an opportunity to witness and praise God. The champion is center stage. Everyone is hanging on every word. Perhaps just as important is how we react and act when we suffer defeat.

No matter who you are, someone is always watching and listening. Are we being Christ–like in defeat or are we complaining and making excuses and being envious of the winner? When Jesus was crucified, Satan thought he had won. But the victory belonged to Jesus, and because of His victory we, too, can rejoice in victory every day and under all circumstances.

†ip

When you use live bait, a kale bend or circle type bend hook will help prevent bass from swallowing your hook.

JOB 23:10

*"But, God knows the way that I take,
and when he has tested me, I will come out like gold."*

A GLOBAL POSITIONING SYSTEM is now a
staple for any serious fisherman. We all have
spots, or waypoints, marked on our GPS units,
and we can go directly to those spots no
matter how far away they are. Even
in dense fog, we can locate an exact
spot. My Humminbird Matrix 97
is in full color and even has an
unbelievable sonar system built
into the unit. It's really a
high-tech marvel.

tip
When fishing
a lying down log,
keep your boat
a little farther away
than usual.

God's Positioning System is even
more remarkable. Not only does He
know where He's going, He knows where I'm
going. He knows all of us, even what we're
thinking. Sometimes our lives seem to be in a dense
fog and we get into situations where we can't see.
Don't worry. Don't panic. God's Positioning System
knows right where we are. Ask Him and He will
lead us safely out of the fog.

JAMES 4:14

But you do not know what will happen tomorrow!
Your life is like a mist. You can see it for a short time,
but then it goes away.

ONE OF MY MOST FRIGHTENING moments as a
teenager on Lake Tenkiller happened on a foggy
morning as I motored my 14–foot aluminum boat
through the fog to run a trotline. I knew the lake
like I knew my own bedroom. Fog was no problem.
I ran wide open toward a point where the line was
tied. Halfway to the point a rock bank suddenly
appeared within a few feet of my bow.
I turned the motor hard but
beached the boat fifteen to
twenty feet up on the bank.
I was unhurt, but scared silly.
Fortunately, I only had a
twenty horsepower Mercury.
I had no idea where I was.
Then the fog went away and I
was no longer lost. God says our life
will also go quickly and we must be
ready for eternity.

tip

Almost every strike
on a jig will come
on the fall.

1 PETER 2:1, 2

So then rid yourselves of all evil, lying, hypocrisy,
jealousy, and evil speech. As newborn babies want milk,
you should want the pure and simple teaching.

DECEIT IS REALLY the basis for all fishing done
with an artificial lure. We're constantly
trying to deceive the fish and make
them believe our lure is really
something very good to eat.
Unfortunately, a lot of life is
handled the same way. So much
of business, advertising, and
personal behavior is shrouded in
deceit. Many people, including
Christians, use deceitful behavior as
a normal means of behavior. This may
work in the short term, but according to
God's word failure is inevitable. When you pray
today, instead of asking God for the usual things
you want, ask God to take away any deceit,
hypocrisy, or backstabbing you have in your life.

†ip

Bass eat crawfish
when their pinchers
are tucked,
not when they are open
in a defensive position.

FEBRUARY 25

MATTHEW 28:20

"I will be with you always, even until the end of this age."

MY DAD AND MY TWO UNCLES, Gene and John, would fish the Ouachita River in Arkansas for catfish in July and August. The hot summer months were best because the river was low and mostly dry and the channel cats would concentrate in deeper holes. We would walk for miles up and down the river searching out these holes. Being impatient, I would always be down the river ahead of the rest. What panic I would feel when I would realize I was all alone and had left my dad and uncles behind. What great relief when I would finally see them coming. Jesus has promised that we need never be alone.

When everyone has deserted us, Jesus is always there.

tip

Fire Tiger
is the bestselling
crankbait
color in the country.

ROMANS 12:6

We all have different gifts, each of which came
because of the grace of God gave us.

A YOUNG MAN ABOUT 9 OR 10 YEARS old asked
me if I had been a professional fisherman since
I was a kid. I told him "no," but that I had loved
fishing since I was old enough to walk. There was
no such thing as pro fishermen until many years
after I graduated from college. Even
then, though, God knew there would
be pros, and He had given me and
others the ability to be
professional bass fishermen.

Realize this: whatever ability
or talent you have has come
from God. He has given you
these abilities to use for His glory.
Use them for that purpose today.

+ i p
Windy banks
on the north and
east shorelines warm up
faster early in
the year.

ISAIAH 41:10

"So don't worry, because I am with you."

WHEN MY GRANDSON Jeremy was about four years old, he decided to take his dog and do a little exploring at a pond near his house. The pond was big and deep, especially for a four-year-old who didn't bother asking or telling anyone about his trip. Much like Jesus' parents when they discovered him missing, Sherri panicked and had everyone else in a panic with her. She called Chris and me at a tournament, and we also were concerned. A frantic hour or so later, Jeremy and his Labrador retriever showed up safe. Was he afraid? Of course not. He had his dog and although he didn't understand it at the time, his God was with him. Such is God's care over His children and their children.

†ip

Keep a lookout for white and blue herons. Fish the same spots where they are feeding.

PSALM 84:11

He does not hold back anything good
from those whose lives are innocent.

IF ONLY I COULD CATCH *some more bass. If only*
I could get that big bite. If only I could win a
tournament. If only I could get a new sponsor.
If only I could turn pro. . . . Life is full of "if onlys."
For a Christian, God has the answer for our
"if onlys." Not just some of the "if onlys," but all
of them. The secret is simply to do what is
right and let God deliver . . . and He will.
He won't necessarily deliver everything we
desire, because not everything we want is a
good thing. God knows the end results, and
He has the power to control everything for
our good. Trust God to do what's best.

tip

Work the edges
of tree lines immediately
after a bass spawn.

March

MARCH 1

JOHN 3:16

*"God loved the world so much that he gave
his one and only Son so that whoever believes in him
may not be lost, but have eternal life."*

THIS IS THE FRONT ROW VERSE to most Americans.
We see the guy with the funny hair hold John 3:16
posters up at many sporting events. I've
even seen him at the Bassmasters
Classic. But it's also the
salvation verse. The entire
gospel of how to be saved is right
there. God loved, He gave, we
believe, and we have eternal
life. We're saved because God
loved us. He gave His Son as
sin to pay for our sin.

When we say we believe,
that means more than simply
believing there is a God or there is a
Jesus. The word "believe" also means trust, among
other things. We trust in Him and we receive life
eternally with God . . . that's how simple the
Gospel actually is. Wow!

tip

With most crankbaits,
you can move to
one size larger
treble hooks.

PROVERBS 14:23

Those who work hard make a profit, but those who only talk will be poor.

IN ORDER TO REALLY LEARN how to catch fish, we must put a lot of work into the game. It is true that many people have a lot of fun just being out on the water, whether they catch a fish or not, but most of us work hard at fishing because of the pleasure and excitement we get when we actually get a fish on the end of our line.

God has instilled in each of us this desire to work hard in order to be rewarded at the end of our labor. In fishing, I believe that the harder I work, the luckier I get. The one thing God does not require us to work for is our salvation. This is God's free gift to us and requires only believing on our part.

tip

White bass, hybrids, and stripers will move to the upper ends of rivers and creeks in early spring.

MARCH 3

JOHN 11:26

"Everyone who lives and believes in me shall never die."

THE FIRST TIME I REMEMBER anything being given to me because of my fishing happened in the late 1960s at a tournament on Lake Sam Rayburn, Texas. John Fox of the *American Angler Television Show* gave me a handful of Mister Twister worms. These were the first plastic worms with a curly tail. I caught a lot of fish on those worms and so did all my buddies. I told everyone how great they were.

God has given us the greatest gifts we can ever receive—eternal life and a joy and hope for everyday living that can never fade away. Yet, so many Christians don't share this gift with their buddies. Today, share what God is doing in your life with a friend. What a great tip that will be.

tip

A spintail bait like a Little George works great in rivers for all species.

PSALM 119:2

Happy are those who keep his rules.

ARE ALL FISHERMEN LIARS or do all liars fish? It is amazing that very few fishermen can tell a fish story without stretching the truth. I've asked hundreds of little kids to show me how big their biggest fish was and invariably they will stretch their hands wide apart.

But sticking to the true stories about life is a gift from God. God laid down laws that He intends for us to obey. These laws are for our own good and were given to create happiness in our life. When we bend the laws we will always create situations that deprive us of our happiness. Sure, we a get away with doing something wrong when no one is looking, but ultimately we'll never be happy with the results.

†ip

Learn to work
a few lures
really well.

MARCH 5

JOHN 13:34

"You must love each other as I have loved you."

FISHING CREATES LONG-LASTING relationships. Like so many other people, some of my best friends are my fishing buddies. One of my wife's closest friends ever was Ricky Green's wife, Bettye, who passed away a couple of years ago. I remember Chris sitting and holding her all night a few days just before she died. You could easily see the love Chris had developed for Bettye over the years of our fishing together.

Jesus tells us the proof that we love Him is that we love one another. This love really needs to surpass any of the other feelings that come into our relationships. Even when another Christian does you wrong, disappoints you, or treats you badly, your response should simply be to love him or her as Jesus loves you.

† i ρ

Use a bobber above a Road Runner to catch crappie over shallow brush piles.

PROVERBS 17:6

Old people are proud of their grandchildren,
and children are proud of their parents.

PROBABLY THE BEST WAY to get your kids and
grandkids into fishing is to take them perch or
bluegill fishing! You can catch bluegill just
about anywhere you can find water.
Teach them how to tie on a hook,
pinch on a split shot and attach a
bobber. Learning to cast,
concentrating on the bobber,
setting the hook, and handling
the fish are just a few of the
important lessons.

tip

Heavy spoons jigged
vertically around
standing timber will produce
cold–water bass.

God created the family, and
then He created fishing as another
means of holding families together. Plan some
time in your schedule in the next couple of weeks
to take your kids or grandkids perch fishing. Resist
all the other more sought–after species. Your family
is well worth the trip!

MARCH 7

ROMANS 14:19
So let us try to do what makes peace
and helps one another.

I RECENTLY FISHED with a thirteen–year–old girl, Tamara, who had won a fishin' trip with me. She's a beautiful young lady who loves the outdoors and loves to fish. That day, however, she put her Terminator spinnerbait in the trees many times throughout the day. I kidded her, singing "George, George, George of the jungle . . . watch out for that tree." Mostly though, I encouraged her and congratulated her on every good cast. (And there were many!) She also caught several good bass. We all make mistakes. We all mess up. God forgives our mistakes and continually encourages us to do better. We need to do the same with each other.

†ip

A prop on a
topwater emulates
extremely small baitfish
on the surface.

ECCLESIASTES 11:1

Invest what you have,
because after a while you will get a return.

AT MY AGE, I'm continually asked why I continue
to fish national bass tournaments. They take
a lot of time and are a tremendous mental
and physical strain on my body, not to
mention the enormous amount of
travel. Of course, I still enjoy the
tournaments and the time with
my friends. And the tournaments
are profitable! The most
important reason is I want to give
back to the game that has given so
much to me. But, just like giving to
God, I can't out-give this game. I've
often tried to out-give God, but He always
gives back more. This is one of God's greatest
principles. Try it for yourself.

+íρ
Use the lowest speed
on your trolling motor that
you can get by with.

MARCH 9

GALATIANS 6:9

We must not become tired of doing good.

CASTING ACCURACY IS really an important part of bass fishing. Just a five percent or ten percent improvement can make a difference in a fisherman's catch. The only way I know to become good is to use good technique and lots of practice. Sometimes it's frustrating to practice hard and seemingly see no improvement, but trust me: practice will make you better.

In life, we also struggle sometimes by always trying to do what's right and good without anybody noticing or caring. We work hard, we help, we give, we love, and we don't receive much in return. God says to never get tired. God's watching and He knows about even the good thoughts we have. Go out and do something good today.

✝ïρ

Use a white buzzbait on warm, rainy spring days

EPHESIANS 4:29

When you talk, do not say harmful things.

I LOVE TO VISIT with the people I'm fishing with
when I am just fishing for fun. Some of my best
days fishing have been with my very good friend
Joe Hall, owner of Blakemore Road Runners.
We talk about everything from our beautiful wives
to politics to business. Sometimes I'm talking about
one thing while Joe is talking about
something entirely different.
Amazingly, we still catch fish.

God gave us the ability to
communicate so we can be
helpful to each other. One of my
most frequent prayers is, "Please,
God, don't let me say anything
bad about anybody." I guess if I
would just concentrate on saying
something good, nothing bad could
come out.

tip
When floating
a stream, don't try to
cover too much
territory in a day . . .
take your time.

MARCH 11

2 TIMOTHY 4:2

Encourage them with great patience and careful teaching.

KIDS DAY ON LAKE TENKILLER is always the first Saturday in June each year. We allow the first 500 kids who sign up to attend. But get this: we have more than 100 volunteers. These volunteers range from teenagers (some who attended Kids Day earlier in their lives) to guys and gals over 70 years old. It's a pure joy to watch them patiently teach and encourage those young kids learning to fish. Believe me, not all of those 500 kids are easy to be patient with. Pause for a moment or two today and think of someone who was encouraging as they patiently taught you something. When you come up with a couple of names, now would be a great time to thank them. By the way, don't forget your mom or dad.

tip

A suspended crankbait will stay in the strike zone longer, producing more fish in cold water.

JOHN 15:19

"But I have chosen you out of the world."

DON BUTLER WON the 1972 Bassmasters Classic
with a bait called an S.O.B. (Small Okiebug).
This is a small crankbait. Many times, early in
the year, a smaller bait will produce a lot of fish.
For one thing, most fishermen in the tournament
were fishing larger spinnerbaits trying to catch
large spawning females. Also, the fish were really
getting a lot of pressure and seeing a lot of
baits. Fishing with something different was
the key to success in that tournament.

God has called us out of the world to be
different. We are to be more loving, more
caring, more joyful, more generous, and
more forgiving than non–Christians.
Some days we fail, but God is
continually working to make our
difference shine.

†ip

Small blades
allow for more
accurate casting.

MARCH 13

ACTS 5:29

"We must obey God, not human authority!"

BASS, CRAPPIE, AND MOST FRESHWATER game fish spawn in the spring and early summer. Many are very predictable because of this annual springtime event that repopulates the waters. We know to fish back in protected pockets and coves. We look for hard bottoms and gentle sloping banks, pea gravel, or sand if we can find them. These spawning fish are following God's laws in order to reproduce and keep their species going. They have no other law to obey, only God's. Man's law in our country is becoming increasingly in conflict with what God has told us to obey. As time goes by, this will become more and more prevalent. In order to prevail, as Christians, we must still obey God's word.

tip

Look for spawning bass behind boat docks and around walkways.

PSALM 103:2

Praise the LORD and do not forget all his kindness.

ALMOST ALL FISHERMEN highly anticipate early spring fishing, but we hardly ever anticipate or remember that most early springs are dominated by high winds. Oh, do we hate fishing in the wind! But the spring wind really is our friend and very beneficial to helping us catch fish. It pushes the warm surface water up on the shorelines (usually the north and eastern shorelines) and warms the water. This brings in the baitfish and the bass that create great fishing. The same wind we hate becomes a blessing. God is working every day in each Christian's life to make all things beneficial. This includes problems, people, and circumstances. Never lose sight of God's blessing in all situations.

tip

Pay very close attention to your water temp gauge in the spring.

DEUTERONOMY 6:7

"Teach them to your children."

CHRIS AND I STARTED our two kids, Jamie and Sherri, working in the family business when they were 9 or 10 years old. We wanted them to learn the kind of effort and work ethics necessary to be successful. We wanted them to learn integrity in business and how to deal with people. We also gave them important jobs to do.

God demands that we teach our kids about Him. We should do this daily. My God is an everyday God, not just a Sunday God. What you teach doesn't have to be some big theological lesson. It can be as simple as talking about some small blessing God gave you that day. What's important is to lead your kids into a working relationship with Jesus.

†ip

A black/chartreuse lizard will produce well during spawning season.

MATTHEW 6:6

"When you pray, you should go into your room and close the door and pray to your Father."

RECENTLY, I SPENT a couple of days fishing with my close friend, Ray Scott, founder of BASS. We spent one evening sitting in his living room until the wee hours of the morning. We were visiting about many years together as bass fishing came from nothing to where it is today. It was a wonderful time as we remembered story after story.

God wants this type of intimate conversations between Him and His children. Public prayer is one thing, but personal prayer is *mano de mano* with the Creator of the universe. How awesome is it that God Almighty actually wants to be involved in this conversation!

† i p
A turtle in the water indicates some underwater brush is nearby.

MARCH 17

JOHN 6:43

"Stop complaining to each other."

ANYONE WHO HAS TAKEN their kids on a fishing trip understands that kids will always fuss with each other. Brothers are bad, but put a brother and sister in the same boat and get ready for some fireworks. This is standard behavior for kids, but unfortunately some carry this temperament throughout their lives. For a Christian, this is totally unacceptable behavior to God.

When God saves us, He places His Holy Spirit in us. The Holy Spirit produces much fruit—including joy—and none of this holy fruit includes grumbling. If you're saved, act like it!

✝ip
Maribou jigs
have more action
in cold water
than plastic or rubber.

PHILIPPIANS 4:6

*Do not worry about anything, but pray and ask God
for everything you need, always giving thanks.*

EARLY SPRING IS without a doubt the very best
time to catch real lunker bass. Bass come out of
the winter season where they have been
almost dormant like couch potatoes.
They get big and fat. Lunker females
bulge with eggs. A fisherman's
biggest concern during the spring
is getting enough time off to go
fishing, but actually catching bass
is nothing to worry about during
this wonderful time of the year.

†ip
Match your
jig colors to the
available baitfish.

　　Having a close relationship with
Jesus allows us the freedom to not
worry about anything at any time of the year.
God has promised to take care of our needs.
He has given us the guarantee of eternal life with
Him and an abundant life here on earth.

PROVERBS 22:4

Respecting the LORD and not being proud will bring you wealth, honor, and life.

I'VE BEEN VERY FORTUNATE to fish with many great fishermen. These include George W. Bush, Davey Allison, Ken Griffey Jr., Toby Keith, Terry Bradshaw, Barry Switzer, and many, many other well–known folks. All of these guys have a lot to be proud of, but I've noted a common thread among them all: they are all very humble. They are quick to give a lot of credit to others and slow to brag on themselves. God tells us that humility is a definite route to success. Humbling ourselves *toward* God is good, but humbling yourself *before* God is what He desires. Whatever your achievement, remember the God who gave you that success.

tip

Switch to a jointed jerk bait if you are missing fish on regular jerkbait.

MARK 5:36

"Don't be afraid; just believe."

WOMEN HAVE BEEN a big part of my fishing life. Chris and I spent a lot of our early dates in a fishing boat, and yes, most of the time we were actually fishing. We pretty much raised our daughter, Sherri, in a bass boat. Now, some of my best days are teaching my six–year–old granddaughter, Jordyn, to fish. But even today, it is still unusual to see two women fishing in a bass boat. Chris and Sherri have never been afraid to go fishing alone, because they know what they're doing under just about any circumstances. They trust their knowledge. God wants us to believe Him and not be afraid no matter what. This trust comes from absolutely knowing that you belong to Him and that He will never forsake you.

†ip

Teach all members of your family, including the kids, how to operate your boat.

MARCH 21

JAMES 5:13

Anyone who is having troubles should pray.

LIGHTNING CAN BE ONE of the most frightening things to happen out on the water. In most lakes, your boat is the tallest thing around and is a sure target for lightning. Some of the hottest storms Chris and I have ever encountered have been on East Texas lakes such as Rayburn, Toledo Bend, and Lake Fork. Your best bet when lightning comes where you're fishing is either to get under a bridge or go to the bank and find cover. Obviously, a lightning storm is one of those good times to pray. For a lot of believers, trouble is the only time they let God work in their lives. God will be there to carry us through our storms, but if we let Him walk with us every day, He will keep us out of most trouble.

tip

A subtle rattle in a crankbait is sometimes better in clear water.

2 THESSALONIANS 3:3
*But the Lord is faithful and will give you strength
and will protect you from the Evil One.*

BASS MOVE TO REALLY HEAVY cover when the
water rises in the spring. A rule of thumb is the
heavier the cover, the bigger the bass. My weapon
to get to these giant females is a jig. One little trick
is to flare the weed guard on your jig. This keeps
you from getting hung up so easily,
but it also displaces the stiffness of
the weed guard to allow for an
easier hookset.

How can we allow God to
work better in guarding us
against attacks from the devil?
Christians and non–Christians
will be attacked by Satan. Without
God, in all honesty, we're pretty
powerless. With God, we have the
power of prayer constantly available.
When Satan attacks, pray! You will be amazed at
how quickly God will come to help.

tip
A sinking worm
with a hook slot
like a Yum Dinger
provides easier
hook sets.

MARCH 23

JEREMIAH 31:33

"I will put my teachings in their minds and write them on their hearts."

PAT TURNER, who shoots camera and runs our production company, has never spent a great deal of time fishing. Sure, he gets to fish for a couple of hours after we finish taping a television show, but most of the time he's just watching through that camera. However, he's also learning and observing, and over the last ten years he has become one the most knowledgeable fishermen in the country. Years of taping and editing *Jimmy Houston Outdoors* has filled his mind with knowledge about this game.

For similar reasons, it's so important for a person to have a daily working relationship with Jesus. This includes prayer, Bible reading, and fellowship with God's people. Try it and before long you'll become far more knowledgeable and will understand what God desires in every circumstance.

✝ip
On your home lake, make sure you fish at least one new spot every day.

PSALM 119:80

*Let me obey your demands perfectly
so I will not be ashamed.*

I LOVE TO SLOW ROLL a Terminator spinnerbait over submerged grass in the early spring. That is where a lot of the big female bass are staging before going shallow to spawn. Try to learn to just barely tick the top of the grass with your bait. Keeping your spinnerbait at just the right depth is the key to catching big strings of big bass, just as keeping God's laws is the key to everything we do in life. Integrity is not something we are born with. In fact, we were born with just the opposite . . . *sin.* No matter what, we must learn to not cut corners when we get in a bind. When a situation arises, ask God to help you rely on His principles. Grow your integrity.

† i p
Don't be afraid to mix and match some wild colors of spinnerbaits, such as a bubble gum (hot pink) head with a chartreuse skirt.

1 JOHN 2:6

Whoever says that he lives in God must live as Jesus lived.

MOST OF US HAVE our ideas and techniques about fishin' developed by the folks we fish with. My skills about trotlining for catfish were learned from my dad and uncles. My kids and grandkids love to fish a spinnerbait. (I wonder where that came from!)

All of us are affected greatly by the people we respect and look up to, so shouldn't what we say about how to live be directed by the greatest person who ever walked this earth? Jesus is that person, and His life was lived in perfection. Today, ask God to give you the mindset of Jesus. Pause in every situation and relationship and give God a chance to let you react like Jesus. Just a two-second pause is all God needs to work miracles if you're serious about letting Him.

†ip

Bass become very active on warm sunny afternoons in the early spring.

JOB 1:22

In all this Job did not sin or blame God.

EVERY FISHING TRIP has its challenges, but if you want even more challenges, jump into a few bass tournaments and see what real fishing troubles are all about.

Sometimes it seems that just getting by day by day is a terrific struggle, but keep in mind that struggles have a benefit. We learn much more at the bottom than we do the top of the heap. It's good to look at challenges as great opportunities to learn and build character. God will actually use these hardships to build you as a Christian. We all know Job as the king of trouble and hardship. When we read about Job the first time, it's almost impossible not to cry for the guy. When we finish the story, we see what God can make out of our troubles. What an awesome God!

tip

Don't overlook shallow stumps as places for bass to spawn.

MARCH 27

PHILIPPIANS 4:4

Be full of joy in the Lord always, I will say again,
be full of joy.

IT'S REALLY EASY FOR ME to have fun fishing.
It's so easy, I can have a lot of fun even when the
fish aren't biting. But what about enjoying the
things that we don't like? What about having fun
during the difficult times? Can we really rejoice in
the Lord always? You bet we can! To me, joy and
having fun is a purposeful attitude that I try to
put on every day. I'm resolved to make it a great
day no matter what. Do I succeed every day? No!
Do I have bad days? Of course! But I am sure of
this . . . anyone can develop this quality of joy.
Get into the habit every day of
asking God to help you do it.
Now go out and have a fun day.

†ip
Use the
lightest slip sinker
as you can
comfortably fish.

EPHESIANS 2:10

God has made us what we are.
In Christ Jesus, God made us to do good works.

THE AREA AROUND ITHACA and Corning,
New York, has some of the best lakes in the
country. They are deep and clear with smallmouth,
largemouth, lake trout, northern pike, and many
other species of fish. These are natural lakes, not
dammed-up rivers and creeks. God created these
lakes for our benefit.

He also created us to help each other.
We are born again in Christ, and God
expects us to do good to each other.
Too much of the time, we become
self-centered and are only
concerned about ourselves.
We live as if we are the only
people who count. We become a
"Me" generation! If you claim
Christ, spend today doing good
works that benefit others.

†ip

Big fish get under
dead water hyacinths
in the early spring.

1 CORINTHIANS 10:23

"We are allowed to do all things"—but not all things are good for us to do.

EVER WONDER WHY you catch so many small bass and not too many big ones? Sure, there are more little ones than lunkers, and a lot of bass get eaten before they have many birthdays, some by bigger bass. The main reason is those older bass are a whole lot wiser. After they've been caught, kissed, and released a time or two, they're pretty hard to fool! Especially if they are caught by a lousy kisser.

We're much like those small bass during our high school and college years. We're out on our own just enough to have the chance to try anything, and some of us do. Like those small bass, our decisions can sometimes cost us dearly. It's critical to live close to God during those years, then maintain that closeness throughout our lives.

tip

Try a crawdad color crankbait on chunk rock banks in late March.

MARCH 30

PSALM 37:7

Wait and trust the LORD.

I WON A BASS-N-RACE tournament at Disney
World in Orlando while teamed up with Bobby
Allison, the great NASCAR legend. Bobby was a
terrific fisherman, especially with plastic worms,
which is what we caught our fish with midway
through that tournament morning. Early
that day they were tearing up a Rebel
Pop-R, but they were usually missing
the bait on the first strike and not
getting hooked until the second or
third bite. These were dynamite
blowups. When the bass struck,
Bobby set the hook. He made up
for it later with worms and we
caught our limit. We won the
tournament and caught Big Bass.

+ip

The longer
you pause a jerkbait,
the more strikes
you generally get.

We all get impatient with God at
times. When you know what a powerful God
He is, you come to expect miracles from Him all
the time. But be patient; it's His timetable.

MARCH 31

NEHEMIAH 2:20
"The God of heaven will give us success."

ABOUT THE EASIEST WAY to catch any species of
fish is with live bait. The really successful guides in
Florida use live bait to produce those giant Florida
bass for their clients. Live bait is so effective, it's not
even legal in bass tournaments.

The way to success with your family, your job
or anything else is with the Living God. He has
been at the core of everything good we have done.
Whatever success we've had in our
family, fishing, or business has come
from God. Yes, there have been
many struggles and trials, but
through my darkest moments
God was not walking with
me—He was carrying me.
What a blessing to live in
God's arms!

tip

Try a small
slip sinker on a
sinking worm like
a Yum Dinger.

April

APRIL 1

JOHN 3:16

"God loved the world so much that he gave his one and only Son so that whoever believes in him may not be lost, but have eternal life."

FISHING A ZARA SPOOK topwater bait is a tiring but productive method of fishing. Sometimes it is critical to work the bait just at the right pace to trigger a strike. Years ago when I was teaching my daughter, Sherri, to fish a Zara Spook, she figured out a way to work the bait with a consistent "walk." She would sing "Jesus Loves Me" and make the bait "walk" back to the boat with the rhythm of that classic children's hymn. Working the bait to the words of that song not only helps you work the bait at the right pace, it reminds you of that wonderful truth—"Jesus loves me, this I know!"

tip

When fishing a topwater, let the bait lie still a few seconds before working it back to the boat.

PHILIPPIANS 4:13

*I can do all things through Christ,
because he gives me strength.*

THE FIRST FIVE MONTHS of the year are killers for
me. I do more than fifty personal appearances, fish
in six to ten tournaments, and tape several fishing
and hunting shows for ESPN and The Outdoor
Channel. Sleep is at a premium. Many nights we
get to bed around midnight or later
only to get back up around four or
five to start all over again. This
takes a huge toll on a person's
mind and body. Most of my
close friends are amazed that
what we do is even humanly
possible. Well, it's not! God
enables me to keep this kind of
schedule. He gives me strength for
my benefit and to serve Him. I find
that the more I serve Him daily, the more
strength He gives me—both mentally
and physically.

tip

Believe you're
going to get a bite
on every cast.

ROMANS 12:2

Be changed within by a new way of thinking.

IF, LIKE ME, you've fished for more years than most other people have lived, you've gained a lot of knowledge and skill about this fishin' game. But this vast amount of experience and know–how can be a trap. We can't keep up if we're not continually learning new techniques and skills both on and off the water.

Similarly, many of us have been Christians for a long, long time. Some of us are growing daily, while some of us are as stagnant as a half–dry creek bed in August. Gradually we become like the rest of the world, living our lives no different than non–Christians. It's really important to read God's word and talk to Him every day. This allows God to continually transform us into the kind of people He want us to be.

tip
Search out clay or mud banks with visible crawdad holes.

PROVERBS 11:24

Some people give much but get back even more.

FISHERMEN GET ON A ROLL sometimes during a
day, or a few weeks or even for months. Jerry Reed
put it in a song: "When you're hot, you're hot!"
Your decision–making is good, your casting is
superb, you're even luckier. When this happens,
relish the moment. One way to stay on a roll is by
giving freely. Giving your money, your time, your
skills, your talents . . . amazingly, your loving
God has promised that the more you give,
the more you will gain. I've tested this
promise over and over and it's never failed.

Do you want more money? Tithe.

Do you want to be a better
fisherman? Give your knowledge and
skills to a kid or someone just
learning to fish.

Give more . . . gain more!

tip

A tiny
"T" Terminator
buzz bait works well
in dead calm water.

LEVITICUS 19:18

"Love your neighbor as you love yourself."

BEFORE THE DAYS of Catch and Release, Chris and I had a way to be very popular with our friends and neighbors. We almost always caught more fish than we could eat, and we pretty much kept everyone we knew supplied in fish. Most of the time, we would filet and bag the fish for them. (Chris can really filet fish!)

Often today many folks don't even know their neighbors, let alone love them. We tend more and more to isolate ourselves from those around us. God never intended this. We help those we love. We encourage and build up those we love. We feed and protect. This is God's will and His design. Reach out and get to know and love a neighbor today, whether at home or at work. God just might make sure they love you back.

†ip

Check the grease in your trailer bearings every three or four months.

MARK 9:37

"Whoever accepts a child like this in my name accepts me."

THERE'S A FISHIN' CLUB near Auburn, New York, that has been doing a kids fishin' day for fifty–two years—FIFTY–TWO YEARS! That's incredible! They've grown over the years and now many grandfathers and even great–grandfathers who attended as youngsters are now helping reach the children. These fishin' days go back four generations. What a great legacy of love those men and women are passing on year after year.

Jesus welcomed the little children. Their minds, hearts, and souls are shaped by God Himself and not yet tainted by the world. We're told to have the faith of a child. Why were the children so important to Jesus? Why should they be so important to us? Because they soon will grow up into moms and dads and grandmas and granddads. Such will inherit the Kingdom of God.

tip

Teach your child
to tie a
really good knot.

GALATIANS 5:22, 23

The Spirit produces the fruit of love, joy, peace,
patience, kindness, goodness, faithfulness,
gentleness, and self-control.

ALL THE BASS PRO SHOP Outdoors Worlds have
huge fish tanks with all kinds of fish. We also
have a large tank in our Jimmy Houston Outdoors
Store on Lake Tenkiller. It's fascinating just to sit
and watch those fish. It doesn't take long to realize
that fish, just like people, have their own
personalities and behaviors. I've often wondered
why some Christians who possess God's Spirit
don't very often exhibit the fruit of that Spirit.
I wonder why we're not happy all of the time.
Maybe it's because we're so
concerned about our own little
wants and needs. The Spirit can't
blossom. Maybe Satan is attacking
our attitudes to keep us from the
Spirit's fruit. Whatever the
reason, I am going to reach up
and grab some of that fruit today.

†ip

Always charge
all your boat batteries
after every use.

JOSHUA 1:9

"Don't be afraid, because the LORD your God will be with you everywhere you go."

MY FIRST ATTEMPT at fishing a tournament in California was Lake Oroville. I borrowed a boat from the local Ranger dealer after flying to the tournament, and then I headed to the lake for the three days of official practice. Oroville was so clear, you could read heads or tails on a dime twenty feet deep. I practiced two days without a bite. On the last day of practice I traveled as far up the river as I could go and began fishing white Road Runners with a half of a pork strip trailer. Throwing at cracks in steep bluffs we started catching bass—lots of bass. During competition I caught more than sixty bass every day and won the tournament by two ounces.

†ip

In the South, most bass will spawn under the March or April full moon.

If you belong to Christ, take heart and be persistent; He is right there even when you seem to be failing.

APRIL 9

PROVERBS 29:11

Foolish people lose their tempers,
but wise people control theirs.

SUBMERGED STUMPS ARE pretty much always
a great place to find a bass. The very best stumps
will be the ones you can just barely see. They're a
little bit deeper, and mostly they get overlooked by
other fishermen. Generally the best technique is to
bump the stump with a spinnerbait. I like a
speed bead Terminator because they're
almost impossible to hang up. Depth
control and direction are finesse
techniques that need to be learned.
God says it's wise to have
another kind of depth
control—self-control. The old
trick of counting to ten before
you speak or react is still as
good as gold. If we will just
pause for a moment when we're
offended or get upset we'll give
God's Spirit the chance to take control
while we stay calm and cool.

†ip
Buy good
fishing line.
The cheap stuff
is a heartache waiting
to happen.

JAMES 1:3

You know that these troubles test your faith,
and this will give you patience.

LEARNING TO CAST a casting reel can try
anyone's patience. For most, it takes a lot of
backlashes and horrible casts before you even
begin to learn. For me it was almost
impossible. The trick is to open the
reel up and keep constant contact
on the spool throughout the
throws. It may take time, but you
can learn.

tip

As the water warms,
you can increase
your speed of retrieve.

Daily trials constantly try
our faith in Jesus and His ability
to handle our problems. We're not
alone. Jesus often admonished His
closest disciples for their lack of faith. These
daily problems are beneficial as they produce
strength for the long haul. As we remain in Jesus
and repeatedly see what He accomplishes in our
lives, we develop the ability to just keep on
keeping on. Have a great day!

APRIL 11

ROMANS 12:3

Do not think you are better than you are.

MY SIX-YEAR-OLD GRANDDAUGHTER, Jordyn, is a hoot to fish and play with. She's really smart and picks up things really quickly. She is like most six-year-olds, determined to do as much as she can on her own. In the boat she is already an expert fisherman, or so she thinks. In her mind, she can pick out the right lure, tie it on, and make a perfect cast. This is pretty acceptable in a child. In fact, we're glad she is so assertive and tries so hard. For the rest of us, this attitude is generally called "pride" and is something God tells us is bad.

It's easy to be humble when you fail, but difficult when you have success. When you win today, glorify God instead of yourself.

tip

Bass located on bluffs are less affected by rising water.

PROVERBS 15:3

The LORD's eyes see everything; he watches both
evil and good people.

UNDERWATER CAMERAS are all the rage now in
fishing. They work incredibly well and are
relatively inexpensive. I own a couple of
these cameras and have seen some
neat stuff when the water was fairly
clear. That's the catch: you need
clear water. Lights help, but clear
water is the deal.

†ip
Search out
pea gravel banks for
spawning crappie.

How would you like to be
able to really, really see everything
underwater? God can.
He can see everything, and He's
watching both you and me right now.
How would we conduct ourselves if we knew God
was sitting right here beside us at work, in our car,
or while we waited in line at Bass Pro or the
airport? I believe we would be a little nicer, happier,
friendlier, and more loving to each other. He is
here! Let's live like it!

1 SAMUEL 6:20

"Who can stand before the LORD, this holy God?"

IT'S A LOT OF FUN TO WATCH people meet some of these superstar fishermen. Most pretty much take these big name guys in stride, but some folks get downright flustered when they get to meet a big fishing star. I once saw a guy get so excited meeting Bill Dance when he introduced his son to Bill, he forgot the boy's name—his son's name, not Bill's. I wonder what this guy might do when he stands before the biggest Name, the Almighty God. How might any of us act, and what can we say and do? The truth is . . . without Jesus we're all in trouble. But praise God, He has provided the way to come before Him. With Jesus we can confidently stand before the throne of God and know we will be welcomed into His family!

+ip

Throw crankbaits when the water level is falling.

JOHN 6:20

Jesus said to them, "It is I. Do not be afraid."

I ONCE HEARD A GUY tell his buddy about his day
with Tommy Biffle. "He put his bait in places we
wouldn't even think of throwing in!" He could
have been talking about any top line pro. They have
the ability and confidence to attempt and make
just about any cast. Learn to cast like this and you
will definitely start catching more bass.

As we go about our day-to-day affairs, we all
face seemingly impossible situations from time to
time. What gives me the confidence to go ahead
and cast when these come along?
My confidence is in Jesus and in my
close personal relationship with Him.
He has always seen me through the
many problem times and He's not
done yet!

†ip

Learn to pitch
and to flip
to get into these
really tough spots.

PSALM 55:22

Give your worries to the LORD,
and he will take care of you.

A BASS ON A BED IS A FISH that is not going to eat anything for several days. For years, most folks thought these fish were next to impossible to catch, but we now have the lures and techniques to catch just about every bedding bass we find. The real trick is simply to worry that bass to death. Eventually the bass will bite. The more patient you become, the more success you will have.

Worries are a major problem in most folk's lives, and worry can cause many major health problems. God knew this all along and gave us His perfect answer to handling our worries . . . give them to Him! No matter how many or how big, get in prayer right now and give your worries to God . . . He will take care of you!

†ip
Saltwater stripers
will move
into rivers to spawn.

MARK 3:25

"A family that is divided cannot continue."

ONE OF MY MAJOR GOALS has always been to
promote family fishing. For the most part, if dad is
involving mom and the kids in his fishing activities,
that family will grow closer. So many positive things
will happen while spending this time together.
Obviously, we are passing on our skills. We also get
into solving problems together, figuring out how to
catch fish, and sharing what God has created
for us to enjoy. If you are not fishing with
your family, you're missing a fantastic
opportunity. Nothing—not tournaments, not
fishing with your buddies—nothing is more
important than the family God gave you.
Take your family fishing the first
chance you get.

†ip

When the
dogwoods bloom,
bass usually will bite
a spinnerbait.

ACTS 2:4

They were all filled with the Holy Spirit.

HAVE YOU EVER NOTICED how some bass seem to put up more of a fight than others? Have you had strikes that nearly jerk the rod out of your hand while other hits are so subtle, you can hardly detect them? One of the reasons for these differences is bass all seem to have distinct personalities. We see this all the time in our large fish tank at our store. God has even created each bass a little differently.

When we are saved and place our complete trust in Jesus, God places in us His Holy Spirit. This Spirit of God noticeably changes the way we act, the way we talk, the way we see others, and even the way we think. All of this is for the better and for our good. God's own Spirit, living individually in each of us . . . WOW!

tip

When the wind
is from the west,
the fish bite
the best!

PROVERBS 14:29

Patient people have great understanding.

I'VE HEARD IT SAID that women make better fishermen than men because they have such great patience. I don't know about that, but I do know my wife, Chris, is the best bass fisherman I have ever fished with. We've been married now for over forty years, so I must be a really patient man myself! (Not exactly.) All my life, I've enjoyed being impatient. I've never prayed for patience in fear that God would give it to me, but supernaturally, after all these years, God has granted me the patience I need even though I didn't request it. At the same time, He has increased my understanding. This enhances my relationship with others and, more importantly, my relationship with Him.

tip

Dingy water allows you to fish closer to the fish.

JOSHUA 23:15

Every good promise that the LORD
has made has come true and in the same way
his other promises will come true.

THE OHIO RIVER around Cincinnati is not known as a great place to fish. In fact, it's pretty much known for just the opposite. A couple of my hunting buddies, Bill Epeards and Jack Gratsch, promised me a great fishing trip if I would do a television show with Jack on the Ohio. I showed up and we fished below one of the locks and dam about twenty miles from the city. We fished Heddon Zara Spooks along the concrete walls below the locks. The hybrid bass fishing was incredible. We caught so many hybrids between five and fourteen pounds that we couldn't keep count. Sometimes it's surprising when a friend's promise comes true, but I can promise you without any doubt. . . . whatever God promises will come true!

† i p

Fish the mouths
of small feeder creeks
that run into a river.

MARK 4:39

*Jesus stood up and commanded the wind and said
to the waves "Quiet! Be still!" Then the wind stopped,
and it became completely calm.*

ALTHOUGH IT'S NOT NECESSARILY the best time
to catch fish, all of us like the magic of a dead calm
lake. Every movement and sound is magnified.
We can hear and see a fish jump a couple of
hundred yards away. Every movement of a
topwater bait sends ripples seemingly forever.
The problem is the fish can see and hear much
better also. Rest assured they know we're there, and
that makes them harder to catch.

Think about the Jesus you believe in.
He can calm a raging sea and
calm the waves. How much
more can He calm the daily storms
we face? This is a God so powerful
He can take the fury out of any
situation we face. Place your full
trust in Him today.

†ip

Most really big
bass live most
of their adult lives around
ten feet deep.

APRIL 21

1 CORINTHIANS 1:25

The weakness of God is stronger than human strength.

HOW MUCH FISHING LINE should you cut off each time you retie? In the tests we did with the Berkley line tester, the line usually would break within six to eight inches of the lure. A good rule of thumb is to cut off one foot of line each time you retie. Always check your line for nicks and frays and rough spots. The weakest spot is your line strength.

How strong is your biggest weakness in life, and how does it control you? Is it money, sex, popularity, power, or something else, and is it ruining your life? If it is, identify the weakness and trade it to God for His power. It's amazing what He can do if you will only let Him. Let God's power be your ruler and your strength.

†ip
Smallmouth like open flats five to eight feet deep after spawning.

HEBREWS 10:25

You should not stay away from the church meetings, as some are doing, but you should meet together and encourage each other.

IT'S AMAZING HOW QUICKLY and easily a bad day fishing can turn into a good one. It's often a tip from another angler that turns the whole day around.

God wants us in church to benefit each other. He intends for us to share our problems and our triumphs, our pain and our joy. He has promised to always be there when we meet to help this along. Will you benefit by showing up at church three or four times this week? Absolutely! Can your presence benefit others? It should. Make it a point to encourage as many folks as you can this week at church. When the week is done, you might just find you've been encouraged most of all!

tip

Use a spinning reel to skip a worm under boat docks.

HABAKKUK 2:5

"Just as wine can trick a person,
those who are too proud will not last."

WHEN YOU'RE FISHING for spawning bass, it really helps to see the fish. Of course, great polarized sunglasses are a must. By seeing the bass, we know better where to place our lures. More importantly is that we are able to determine the attitude of the fish. This gives us clues as how to try to catch that bass or maybe to not even attempt a particular fish. Pride can affect us like fishing without polarized sunglasses; it makes our vision of life cloudy and makes us miss the mark in our actions. Pride can blur the really important things in our lives and turn us into people no one wants to be around. Rest assured, this is one of Satan's greatest tools to destroy us. Ask God today to help you battle this adversary!

tip

The only difference in a major or minor feeding period is length of time.

PROVERBS 15:4

Healing words give life, but dishonest words
crush the spirit.

MY SON, JAMIE, and I catch and haul shad to our
private lake to help feed the fish. It's a difficult
and delicate job because shad die so easily.
We've learned many tricks, but the best
is adding stock salt to the water.
Before the salt, the shad look all
fuzzy and sick. Add the salt and
they become sleek and healthy.
Words of hope, encouragement,
and joy are like adding salt to a
shad tank. They bring life and
healing back to a hurting soul.
We know individuals who bring those
words into every conversation with everyone
they meet. How great it would be if we would all
strive to be one of those individuals. I'm sure going
to try. How about you?

† i p
Watch the birds.
They will show you
where the baitfish are.

ISAIAH 62:5

As a man rejoices over his new wife,
so your God will rejoice over you.

WE ALL LIKE TO TALK about the good old days in fishing. We remember all the great strings of bass, crappie, and catfish we caught. Most of my best fishing memories involve my wife, Chris. After more than forty years of marriage, I love her now more than ever, and I thank God every day for picking her out for me. It's impossible for us to realize how much God really loves us. Everything He has done from creation until now has been done out of His love for those He created.

It's exciting to think we can put a smile on God's face. What makes God smile? Talking to Him, reading His word, praising and worshiping Him? Sure . . . but maybe most of all . . . living our lives by the example His Son, Jesus, set for us.

tip

Teeny crankbaits will produce sometimes when all else fails.

LUKE 19:10

"The Son of Man came to find lost people
and save them."

WE USE BAITS NOW with scents, taste, and salt.
All of these help us catch fish. One downside
with tubes, sinking worms, and wacky worm rigs,
though, is that a lot of fish swallow the hook.
I fish most of the time with barbless hooks.
Even when a bass swallows the bait
and hook, I can remove it without
killing the bass. God's desire is that
we all be saved by His Son, Jesus.
Jesus accomplished much on this
earth, performed great miracles
and taught tremendous life
lessons. His purpose, however,
was to die on that cross to pay for
your sins and mine. He rose again
to life to prove we could also be saved
from death and live forever with Him. He has
forever removed the barbs of sin and death.

tip

Search out points
in submerged weedlines
with your depthfinder.

JOB 41:11

"No one has ever given [God] anything that [He] must pay back."

WE SPEND A LOT OF MONEY and invest a lot of time trying to become better fishermen and catch more fish. We all get excited when we hear about a new lure or technique. We're making this investment in hopes of a greater return in fish catches. We often play the same game with God. We mentally expect to get what we want and receive His blessings in abundance. After all, we tithe, we teach, we attend, we witness, we support . . . Doesn't God owe us something in return? Not at all. Everything we have, including our money, time, and talents, are already gifts from God's love. What we choose to give back to Him must be from our love to Him!

tip

Follow up missed buzzbait strikes with a slow rolled spinnerbait or tube.

1 SAMUEL 10:9

When Saul turned to leave Samuel,
God changed Saul's heart.

I FIRST MET GEORGE W. BUSH when his dad was vice–president under Ronald Reagan. We first fished together when he was running for governor of Texas. Perhaps his most enduring quality is how genuine he is . . . what you see is what you get. President Bush wears his faith in God on his sleeve and has taken much criticism for this. I remember him once saying God changed his heart. Fact is, that's exactly what God does when we turn our lives over to Him. If you're not really the kind of person you want to be, the heart is the place to start. Most of us don't have a clue about making this change. The master heart surgeon is standing by right now, just waiting on your call to Him.

tip

Wake a spinnerbait
on rip–rap
early in the morning.

APRIL 29

HEBREWS 11:1

Faith means being sure of things we hope for
and knowing something is real even if we do not see it.

THE EASIEST WAY to get a mental picture of an underwater creek or roadbed is with ten to twelve marker buoys. Crisscross over the creek or road, drop a buoy each time you cross. Quickly, you have the creek or road laid out with buoys on the top of the water. Now you know what it looks like and can easily see key areas to fish. This increases our faith in the particular structure. I'm not sure there is a shortcut to real faith in Jesus. If there is, it's the fact that God chose us and He's working in us and for every day. We don't see God, but we see His results. Just like we're really not seeing that creek; we're only seeing marker buoys, but we know the creek is there. I see God's work and I know Jesus is there.

†ip

Crawdads will
reappear in the
early fall as food
for the fish.

ACTS 20:35

*"I taught you to remember the words Jesus said:
'It is more blessed to give than to receive'."*

WIVES OF TOURNAMENT FISHERMEN must be a
special class of women. What a demanding job and
what a great asset to any tournament angler.
Chris helps drive the rig to the tournament,
practices with me, helps locate fish, keeps my boat
clean, and winds new line. All this before the
tournament even starts. Many wives homeschool
the kids while on the road. All this and each wife
is still her husband's biggest encourager and
number one fan. Why do these ladies
do all this giving? Love! Each
woman loves her fisherman, and
her blessing is helping him and
seeing him do well. God loves us
enough to give His Son to save us
from an eternity in hell. His
giving enables us to come before
Him clean of sin and ready to
spend forever in paradise.

tip

The calmer the water,
the slower you need
to work your topwater.

May

MAY 1

PSALM 32:5

*I confessed my sins to you and didn't hide my guilt. . . .
and you forgave my guilt.*

IN A RECENT BASS TOURNAMENT one of my
close friends, Mark Menendez, broke one of the
tournament rules. Although no one knew except
Mark, he turned himself in to tournament officials
and was disqualified. Mark showed great integrity
but still paid the price. He didn't cheat; he
simply violated a rule by accident. We all
violate God's rules. And yes, these
violations carry a penalty. God knows
every time we sin. We're not telling
Him anything new when we
confess our sin; what we are
doing is humbling ourselves
before God. This is what God
requires. This is where my
God gets really great. He
forgives my violation, erases my
guilt, and does not disqualify me.

† i p
Small edges
of shade along
bluffs will hold fish.

JOHN 6:27

*"Work for the food that stays good always
and gives eternal life."*

FISHING IS JUST A GAME, but if you ever want
to get really good at this game, you've really got
to put in a lot of work. This comes pretty easy
for most of us because of our passion
for fishing. We get up early and
spend hours standing and making
cast after cast. It's hard work, but
we love it because we love fishing.
The work God is asking is that
we believe in His Son, Jesus
Christ. The food that produces
eternal life is prayer, reading God's
word, and assembling with God's
people. We often try to feed our spiritual
hunger with worldly food, music, entertainment,
movies, and the like. This leaves our souls hungry
and our hearts empty. Fill up today with the food
of love. If Jesus can feed five thousand people on a
mountaintop, He can certainly feed you and me.

tip

Always wear
polarized sunglasses
while fishing.

MAY 3

2 KINGS 20:5

"I have heard your prayer and seen your tears, so I will heal you."

MAY IS ONE of the really great months to fish in most of America. You have fish in pretty much all stages of the spawn, and you can catch bass in a variety of ways. Pick your favorite lure and technique, put your foot on your Minn Kota, and get after it. At the end of day, you should have some great string–stretching memories. If only May could last forever. God has allotted each of us only so many Mays and just a certain number of days. Through King Hezekiah, God gives us an example of adding to one's life. It's one of my favorite Bible stories as God adds years to the king's life. What a great example of the power of prayer. Proof positive, God answers prayer and nothing is too tough for Him to handle.

tip

Jerkbaits, such as Rogues, produce well over deeper points after the spawn.

JOSHUA 8:1

The LORD said to Joshua. "Don't be afraid or give up"

MUDDY WATER SCARES a lot of bass fishermen. When you look at water with coon tracks on top, it can be pretty frightening. The bass, on the other hand, don't mind at all. They're well equipped with great senses to survive in muddy water. They actually can see much better than you can imagine. We need to remember three key things— shallow, shallow, shallow.

†ip
Occasionally check and tighten the lug nuts on your boat trailer.

The shallower you fish, the more bites you'll get. Jesus continually told His disciples not to be afraid. He knows that fear is a natural response. We are not sure about what's going to happen in a scary situation. Our comfort is that Jesus does know the outcome. He also knows that He will help us and see us through. In fact He will even bring us through death itself.

MAY 5

TITUS 2:2

Teach older men to be self-controlled, serious, wise, strong in faith, in love, and in patience.

IT'S AMAZING HOW MANY youngsters are taught to fish by their granddads. It's true, granddads probably have more time, but mostly they have great teaching qualities. I know of no dad who is as patient and self-controlled with his kids as their grandfather is with them. This is designed by God. As we grow older, God is at work building us into the men He desires us to be. As you look through the qualities in the scripture above, measure each one in yourself. If you find that you're lacking any or all of the attributes, ask God specifically to help you. You'll find that He will supernaturally. After all, that's what He wants for you anyway.

tip

The bigger the crankbait, the bigger the bass.

ROMANS 12:11

*Do not be lazy but work hard, serving the Lord
with all your heart.*

THE JACK HOUSTON MEMORIAL FOCAS
Tournament is one of the biggest events in
Cherokee County each year. It starts with a gospel
singing and a great Outdoors Challenge on Friday
night and a huge bass tournament on Saturday
where we give away over $50,000 in
cash and prizes. The grand finale is
FOCAS Sunday at Keys Baptist
Church. This special service
always sets the attendance record
for the year. This event has
literally thousands of hours of
work involved. The work starts
months in advance and is done by
our friends and staff. Nobody gets
paid. We're just serving our Lord.

If you really love Jesus, make sure you're
serving Him every day. God has especially equipped
us all to serve, and possibly nothing disappoints
Him more than our failure to serve Him.

tip
Take time
to learn how
to interpret your
fish locators.

1 PETER 4:12

My friends, do not be surprised at the terrible trouble which now comes to test you.

CHRIS AND I FOUND a little patch of fish one week on a small flat on the bed of a creek. The spot was only about fifty yards long but was loaded with good bass. For three straight days we caught six to ten bass every time we fished this special honey hole. Then it rained four or five inches. The lake came up six feet and we couldn't buy a bite on that spot.

The Bible tells us we will have terrible times come along. Most all of us have already been there and know they will come again. That's just how life is. How do we make it through these tests of reality? We make it by God's amazing grace. He has mountains and mountains of grace just waiting to be given to His chosen ones. When terrible trouble happens, God will always be right there on the spot with enough amazing grace to see us through.

†ip

Search out small city lakes for some surprising good fishing.

MATTHEW 25:45

"'I tell you the truth, anything you refused to do even for the least of my people here, you refused to do for me'."

IT'S A HELPLESS FEELING to break down on the water. Sometimes you're miles from where you launched, floating around with no help in sight. What a relief when you see a boat coming. What a sinking feeling when the driver doesn't see you or pretends not to see you and looks the other way. Fortunately, most folks will stop and give you a tow. Unfortunately, we do live in a society where we increasingly look the other way. Jesus says that when we do this, we are turning our backs on Him. Jesus went out of His way to help those who needed help the most. He expects us to do the same. When you look at someone in need, you're actually looking into the face of Jesus. As people of Christ, we should be first in line to help.

†ip

Use a bobber to suspend a Road Runner over submerged brush piles.

LAMENTATIONS 3:25

The LORD is good to those who hope in Him,
to those who seek Him.

FINDING FISH AFTER THEY SPAWN can be pretty difficult. The fish don't necessarily stay shallow, but they won't automatically go deep. Most suspend four or five feet deep, but this can be in a wide variety of places depending on the type of water you are fishing. They might be in over thirty feet of water on points or in the tops of willow trees at five or six feet deep. You get the picture? Finding God is much easier and is constant no matter where you are or who you are. God is right there with you right now. All you need to do is to seek Him. Get in prayer and talk to God, get personal and intimate with Him. Pretty quickly you'll start to see just how good the God you hope in really is.

†ip

Illinois pond weed
(duck weed)
has thick stems
that provide
great underwater cover.

JUDGES 10:15

*"We have sinned. Do to us whatever you want,
but please save us today."*

LAKE HAMILTON IN HOT SPRINGS, Arkansas,
is one of the city lakes that has super fishing. One
of the overlooked fisheries here is catfish. Because
Hamilton is a high usage lake with lots of houses,
restaurants, and marinas, it has tons of lights.
These lights are a great attractant for bugs and
baitfish. Make a bet, the catfish will show up pretty
much every night.

Our sins are out in the light 24/7 to God.
Nothing we do is hidden from Him. Knowing this,
why should we even try to hide our sins from
God? Our sins create consequences and
produce bad results. These bad
situations will continue until we
put ourselves under God's control
and will. Yes, we will be
punished for our sins, and then
only God can and will save us.

tip

Catfish will feed
under gar rolling
on top during
spawning season.

MAY 11

EXODUS 23:2

*"You must not do wrong just because
everyone else is doing it."*

HAVE YOU NOTICED that when a hot new lure
comes out, it's not long until every other company
has one just like it! Sometimes the imitations sell
better and catch more fish than the original.
This is indeed a copycat business. Unfortunately
this need to imitate is a by–product of human
nature. We tend to follow the group whether it's
right or wrong, moral or immoral. One of the
biggest breakdowns in our morality and values is
that if everyone is doing it, it must be okay.
The truth is, wrong is wrong, and right is not to be
compromised just because everyone
else does. Our values, our morals, or
rules for life come from God.
As God's people we simply must
live by God's law and not be
swayed by the thinking and
actions of everyone else.

†ip

Black perch
make great trotline bait
for large early
season catfish.

MARK 10:45

"The Son of Man did not come to be served.
He came to serve others."

WE DO A LOT OF ENTERTAINING on our ranch in
southern Oklahoma. Some of it is for business,
but most is just sharing with our friends. Chris
cooks and serves great meals, and we work extra
hard to make their visits special. Some people,
because of age or physical limitations, we have to
help get in the boat. We tie on hooks, we rig
baits, land and unhook fish, pick out
backlashes . . . etc. Sometimes we even
throw the lure out for the beginning
anglers. We do this because we
love these friends. All of them
have shown a special love for us,
and seeing them happy is
our reward.

tip
Screw down
a magnet on your
front deck to
hold your needle nose
and cutters.

Jesus has a special love for
each of us. His desire is to serve our
every need, not for just a day or week
. . . not for a lifetime, but for eternity.

MAY 13

PHILIPPIANS 2:1

Does your life in Christ give you strength?

THE MORE YOU FISH, the stronger you become in certain muscles you use in fishing. Your legs, your arms, your wrists . . . well, that's the theory, but the older you get the more you prove this premise wrong. I'm fishing now more than at any time since college, yet it seems I hurt now more than ever.

But I know that without the work of fishing, I'd be in nowhere near as good a shape.

God wants us to keep ourselves strong. He really intends for our lives to be filled with strength and power. The strength to overcome all of life's ups and downs. The strength to succeed when failure seems inevitable. This is what life in Christ is all about. My God delivers when everything else I've relied on has failed. God doesn't dump this strength on us in one big pile. He gives it out just as we need it.

†ip

In extremely heavy cover, mash your barbs down on a Road Runner.

2 TIMOTHY 1:7

God did not give us a spirit that makes us afraid,
but a spirit of power and love and self–control.

ONE OF THE TRICKS to fishing heavy cover is
short casts. This knowing how to pitch and flip
comes in handy. The fish are so secure in
heavy cover, we can get in really close
and not spook them. God places His
Holy Spirit in us to keep us from
fear. He gave us this Spirit of
confidence and power. God's
power. His Spirit also produces
benefits—love and self control.
How do we get this amazing
Spirit? Can we order it off television?
How much do we pay? Are there
shipping and handling charges? Actually God
gives this Spirit of power, love, and self–control to
everyone He saves. This is the "*wait—there's more*"
part of salvation. Ask God to let His Spirit work in
you today.

tip

Practice flipping
and pitching
with a coffee cup.

MAY 15

PROVERBS 15:4

Dishonest words crush the spirit.

WE'VE GOT HUNDREDS of bluegill and perch that hang out at our dock. My grandkids, Jordyn and Kyle, love to catch these fish. They like to use Berkley Crappie Nibbles. This is a prepared Power Bait that we use to tip Road Runners. With a small hook, it's dynamite for these small panfish. The problem is that the little ones steal the bait often without the kids knowing they had a bite.

There's a little built-in larceny in everyone. The devil uses this to hurt others, especially in what we say. Words can be more damaging than physical pain. If the truth hurts, how much more a lie? Be extra careful to not let Satan lead you into a falsehood. After all, God wants us to build up, not crush.

tip
Rattles often produce extra bites on a plastic worm.

JONAH 4:6

The LORD made a plant grow quickly up over Jonah,
which gave him shade.

RECENTLY I HAD THE PLEASURE of fishing with
two young men from *Hunt of a Lifetime,*
Trevor and his brother, Cody.
Both of these guys are really good
fishermen and very competitive.
Because of a recent bone marrow
transplant, Trevor could only stay
out in the sun for short periods of
time. The forecast for our outing
was 90 degrees and sunny, but the
first morning it rained so hard, we
couldn't even fish until noon!
The sun did peek out a time or two, but
not for long. The second morning it was
crystal clear at 6:30 a.m. By 7:30 a few clouds
rolled in, and by 8 o'clock, solid clouds and a light
rain. We caught more than a hundred bass those
two days. Does my God care enough about one
12–year–old boy to send those needed clouds?
You bet your last rod and reel He does!

tip
Go early,
stay late.

MAY 17

1 THESSALONIANS 4:16

The Lord Himself will come down from Heaven
with a loud voice.

BOB FERRIS WAS the booming voice of Bass'n Gal
for twenty–one years. He had one of those voices
that was almost a melody when he spoke; he was
almost singing. In addition, his voice really carried.

When Jesus returns, it literally will be the
shout heard around the world. Every man, woman,
and child—inside or outside—will hear the voice
of Almighty God. Indeed, all mankind will
tremble. Many will try to run and hide. Some
really won't understand what is happening. For
those of us who have received redemption
from that same Jesus, it will
be the moment of ultimate
victory. And, yes, I sure would like
to still be alive here on this earth to
experience that moment.

†ip

As you move
into warmer weather,
use smaller worms.

MAY 18

MATTHEW 15:28

Jesus answered, "Woman, you have great faith!
I will do what you asked."

AS A KID, I pretty much tried to beg into every
fishing and hunting trip my dad went on. He took
me fishing most of the time, but hunting trips
took more asking. Dad did start taking me way
before I was big enough to carry a gun, and as I
grew older Dad's answer was almost
always "yes".

As we grow as believers in
Christ, we also grow in faith that
God will answer our requests
with a "yes". When this
happens, you'll notice yourself
including God in the smaller
matters in your life, not just
major problems. That's just what
God wants. In fact, He demands it.
Realize that God, in order to be your God,
must be involved daily in all the facets of your life.
Only then can God's will really be done.

tip
Spray Reel Magic
on all your
electrical connections
in your boat about
once a month.

HEBREWS 4:15

When [Jesus] lived on earth, he was tempted in every way that we are, but he did not sin.

A WARM, BEAUTIFUL SPRING DAY to a fisherman is like a picnic basket to Yogi Bear. Old Yogi would do just about anything to get that basket. We'll do pretty much anything to go fishing on one of those "special" days! And, yes, I've skipped class, work, responsibilities, and even church to go fishing.

Surely almost all of us can identify here. Jesus walked on earth more than thirty years as man. He faced the same daily temptations of any man, yet He remained God and faced these temptations without sinning. His power? His Father's word! Whatever temptation confronts you today, and you will be confronted by something, God's word can also be your power. The more immersed we are in the word, the more capable we become to handle temptations.

†ip
After a rain you can stock up on nightcrawlers in most city parks without having to dig.

NUMBERS 11:29

"I wish the LORD would give His spirit to all of them!"

IT'S WILD SOMETIMES to watch some sort of live bait fall into the water . . . a crawfish, frog, grasshopper, spider, and the like. We expect a fish to instantly explode on the real thing. Sometimes it happens, but often the bait safely reaches shore. It succeeds by trying to not look like or act like a crawfish, frog, grasshopper or spider. Ironically, we're trying to make our artificial bait look and act like the real live bait. Satan, along with all his followers, was thrown from Heaven for trying to be God. Isn't it amazing that God had already planned to give His Holy Spirit to those who would believe in His Son, Jesus. Awesome!

†ip

Add a rattle
to your spinnerbait
in muddy water.

EXODUS 16:11

"Then you will know I am the LORD your God."

ONE OF THE THINGS that bugs me the most is letting a fish swallow the hook on a plastic worm or tube. Barbless hooks make it easier to get the hook out without harming the bass. I hate killing bass! The problem is knowing when there's a fish on the line. This is especially difficult in grass such as coontail. Some strikes are so subtle and some bass, especially the big ones, suck in the hook so quickly.

The grace of God is on the line; our Lord has been missed and not recognized by a lot of mankind throughout the years. Even as He walked on earth, most people did not know He was the Christ. Just as today, many know about Him but deny Him. God desires that all know Him as Lord as He is still at work today drawing us to Himself.

†ip

When in doubt . . .
set the hook!

MATTHEW 22:37

"'Love the Lord your God with all your heart,
all your soul, and all your mind'."

CHRIS GOT TICKLED at our granddaughter,
Jordyn, recently. You see, she's almost seven and
has already caught lots of fish. As she was catching
bluegill after bluegill one day she looked up at
Chris and said, "Grandma Chris. I just love fishing
here at Twin Eagle [Ranch]." She was having a
terrific time.

There are many facets to what we call love.
What does God want? I believe God desires the
most complete love we can imagine. A love that
rises above material things, hobbies, careers,
even family. Do we really love God that
much? How can we? By understanding
that all else we love is a gift from
God. Without God's love for us
and His mighty blessings,
we have nothing, including our
next breath.

tip

A fish feeder
will enhance your
fishing in any
body of water.

GALATIANS 6:2

By helping each other with your troubles,
you truly obey the law of Christ.

FISHERMEN ARE BOTH THE BEST and the worst
when it comes to helping. The same guy who will
stop and tow a total stranger with motor problems
will lie to his best friend about where and how he
is catching fish and what on! What's wrong with
that picture? Well, it's all about agendas. We know
we need to reach out and help, but we're only
willing to serve if it doesn't affect our agendas or
successes. Our friend is a threat to our own fishing
success. The stranger is not. The agenda of Jesus
was not only to help, but to *solve* the troubles of
others. Jesus put the problems of
others above His own. Helping each
other is a form of obedience to God,
and He really knows how to bless
us when we are obedient to Him.

†ip

When cleaning a lot
of crappie or white bass,
set the trigger to Constant
on your fillet knife.

HEBREWS 12:14

Try to live in peace with all people,
and try to live free from sin.

WE PLAY IN A SPORT where there's not much
confrontation among competitors. Unlike most
sports where intense rivalry, verbal abuse, and even
fights happen regularly, tournament fishing is
pretty tame. However, some of the younger
fishermen get out of line occasionally, and a few
get bent out of shape if they believe someone is
saying something negative about them.
This is simply ego, but it's a tool the
devil uses to destroy peace and
harmony. Pride is an especially easy
and effective sin that can snowball
into more and more sins. One of
the best things any of us can do
is humble ourselves and go make
peace with someone we believe we
have a problem with. I think God
will bless those in a mighty way.

✝ip

There are more
fish in any given spot
than you think.

MAY 25

REVELATION 22:15

"Outside the city are the evil people, those who do evil magic, who sin sexually, who murder, who worship idols and who love lies and tell lies."

WHAT ARE YOU GOING TO DO when you retire? To a lot of us, including me, retirement means we're going fishing. I've got many retired friends who fish almost every day. Almost everyone I know who is about my age is retired. The rest of us are dreaming of all those great spring days ahead when we'll fish away our retirement. The ultimate retirement, though, is not something that will last fifteen to twenty years, or even a hundred or a thousand years—it's forever! And we have only two places to spend that "forever"—Heaven or hell. My God has made it pretty plain about who will spend their forever retirement with Him or elsewhere. He's left the choice up to us. I know He's guaranteed my retirement in Heaven with Him. How about you?

† i p
If you can get just one bass in a school to bite, it often starts a feeding frenzy.

JEREMIAH 18:11

*"'Stop doing evil. Change your ways
and do what is right'."*

MOST FISHERMEN THINK they're pretty good at
catching fish. Most believe if they really had the
chance they could make it big on the pro
level. Most could not. But what they
believe in their own minds is what
is important.

Over the years we've blurred
the lines in our minds between
"good" and "evil" to the point
where there is not much
difference, but God draws a very
well–defined line between good and
evil. To God, it's adultery—not "well,
everyone does it." To God, it's murder—not a
woman's choice. To God, it's a lie—not just
bending the truth a bit. To God, it's divorce—
not incompatibility. To God, it's stealing—not "I
can't afford to tithe." It's time we wake up as a
people and start doing right according to God.

†ip

Watch for the
mayfly hatch,
and fish near bushes
and docks
with mayflies.

PSALM 104:9

You set borders for the seas that they cannot cross.

TIDAL WATERS HAVE ALWAYS presented a challenge
for me in bass fishing. Just about the time I think
I've figured it out, the tide beats me again.
The one thing that seems pretty constant is that
low tides are better while high tides are difficult.
Isn't it amazing how the tides work, how timely
they are, and how predictable? What a mighty God
who can control these huge bodies of water and
move them up and down, in and out,
on a daily basis. God never says "oops"
and allows the tide to rise another
twenty feet. He is precise with
these gigantic bodies of water.
We've got faith enough to
build homes and business right
on the waterfronts.
Recognizing this power is the
beginning to the understanding
of how powerful God really is.

tip

Take pictures
of water at low levels
to know where
to fish when it rises.

ISAIAH 25:4

You protect the poor; you protect the helpless
when they are in danger.

PEACOCK BASS FISHING is probably the most
exciting freshwater fishing you can do. I've
fished giant Guri Lake in Venezuela many
times for peacocks. It rains some almost
every day, but violent storms are rare
and usually end well before dark.
One time, Chris, Sherri, and I
were caught twenty–five miles up
the lake right at dark in an
extremely violent storm.
We traveled those miles in two tiny
boats with no lights, no bilge pumps
. . . in total darkness. The storm was
hot. The waves were the biggest I have ever
seen, and we were never close to shore. It took
more than four hours of impossible boating,
but somehow our family made it. At the time,
I thought our odds of safety were almost zero,
but my God gave us His protection and made
those odds one hundred percent.

tip

Fish a silver spoon
fast through
schooling bass.

MAY 29

MARK 13:13

*"Those people who keep their faith until
the end will be saved."*

I RECENTLY MADE AN APPEARANCE for Ranger
Boats in Virginia. We were to arrive in Roanoke,
take the shuttle to the hotel, and be ready to work
the next morning. My day had started at 5 a.m.,
and I was looking forward to a good night's sleep
ahead. My last plane was late, so we arrived at
12:30. The hotel shuttle had closed. No taxi in
sight. Called a taxi and waited for thirty minutes
for that . . . no problem. In my room by 1:45
a.m.—a smoking room. I've never smoked a
cigarette in my life and couldn't breathe.

Back to the front desk—no
non–smoking rooms available.
As I unpacked, no razor and no
shaving cream. Ugh. In bed by 2:30
a.m. I slept with the outside door
wide open and the air conditioner
on high. Throughout it all,
I continually asked God to keep
me Christlike—and He did.

tip

Match your
crankbait color to
the color of the
dominant baitfish.

LUKE 11:4

"Forgive us for our sins, because we forgive everyone who has done wrong to us."

A TWO- OR THREE-POUND BASS can break fishing lines several times its weight. What generally keeps this from happening is a small amount of line stretch (forgiveness) built into monofilament and the small forgiveness in our rod tips. As long as you can keep the fish from getting a straight pull on you, you'll usually land the fish.

A small amount of forgiveness can solve big, big problems in most relationships. Just as important, a little forgiveness can keep tiny problems and mess-ups from festering into major issues. The devil hates it when you forgive. You can ruin his day anytime with forgiveness. When you do, God steps in and rewards you with His blessings. In fact, you will feel better and receive more than the person you forgave.

tip
Try swimming a tube through suspended baitfish.

MAY 31

1 CORINTHIANS 6:13
The body is not for sexual sin but for the Lord . . .

THE ORIGINAL HEDDON ZARA SPOOK is a bait you need to sort of work yourself into. By this I mean . . . fish it for a few minutes at a time, extending the time as you go. It will take a while, but you'll soon be able to "walk the dog" with a Spook all day if necessary. We actually strengthen the exact muscles needed to fish this bait.

†ip

Spotted bass like rock piles and humps.

God perfectly created our bodies to be able to do certain things. He also warns about all types of sins that will destroy the bodies He created. Pre–marital sex and adultery can lead to sexually transmitted diseases, such as AIDS, that have devastating effects on our bodies. God created our bodies to do wonderful things for us and for Him. Let's keep them that way.

June

1 TIMOTHY 5:25

Good deeds are easy to see, but even those that are not easily seen cannot stay hidden.

MOST OF US REALLY LIKE to brag when we've done something good. Probably no national bass tournament ever has been won without some local angler telling anyone who would listen that he told the winner where to fish or told him about the winning lure. When we do good, we really don't need to be concerned about being noticed or getting a pat on the back. God sees, God knows, and God has promised to reward every good deed. I think He probably has a greater reward for those good deeds we keep secret than those everyone knows about. Try to do something especially good today and keep it just between you and God. Then wait and see what happens.

tip

Locate points on submerged weed lines. These can be real sweet spots.

TITUS 3:6

God poured out richly upon us that Holy Spirit
through Jesus Christ our Savior.

FEW FISHERMEN CAN DENY there is a God. Look around at any body of water on an early summer day. The steam rises, baitfish dimple the surface, and an occasional explosion signifies a big bass having breakfast. A deer with a spotted fawn walks along the shore. The best fisherman of all, a blue heron or kingfisher, catches yet another bluegill. Glancing up, a redtail hawk circles. Look higher and an American bald eagle soars. Can you feel it? Can you feel God's Spirit in you? Oh, what rushes this God of ours shares!

†ip
Use a black bucktail skirt on your spinnerbait at night.

JUNE 3

PROVERBS 12:10
Good people take care of their animals.

I HAVE A REAL PASSION for the fish in our private
lake and for the deer and turkey on our land.
When the lake floods, Chris and I go to the
"hole" below the dam and catch the bass that
have gone through the spillway tube. If we don't,
they'll die of starvation. We catch these bass and
put them back in the lake. If you have a body of
water you fish . . . a pond or a creek . . . take care
of it! God expects you to take care of the creation
over which He gave you dominion. Even if you
don't own the water but merely have permission
to fish, put out a feeder, feed the fish, fertilize the
water. If we take care of the little
places we fish, we will have lots
more and bigger fish to catch.

tip
Shad concentrate
in certain sections
of a creek.
Find the shad,
find the fish.

JOB 38:36

Who put wisdom inside the mind or
understanding in the heart?

HOW MUCH OF FISHING is luck and how much
is skill? Just like any other activity or sport, luck
does play a part in any given day's success, but
luck alone will not make you a good fisherman.
You need skill, knowledge and an understanding
of the fish, water, weather, and a few other
factors. God has given us the ability to gain
these assets. We have more available to us
now than ever to help us improve, but
perhaps nothing helps us more than
getting out on the water and
putting our information to
work. On your next fishing trip,
take along someone you've never
fished with and pay close
attention. You both will learn.

†ip

When wading,
shuffle your feet to
avoid dropoffs.

JUNE 5

1 KINGS 3:25

*"Cut the living baby into two pieces and
give each woman half."*

ANYONE WITH BASIC KNOWLEDGE of the Bible
knows the end of this story. The mother of the
living baby would rather give up the baby than see
it die. The mother of the dead baby would just as
soon see the living baby die—it's not hers and if
she can't get what she wants, then no one else
should either. What are we willing to give up
in order to get what we want? Like the
mother of the dead baby, most people
are willing to give up what they
believe if it means they get their
way. Our values really mean
nothing if we are willing to
compromise them. Most of us
have opportunities every day
to show those around us what
we stand for and what we believe.
All too often I'm guilty of not
standing on the firm ground God has
given me. How about you?

†ip

A Hamby
keel protector will
enhance the
resale value of your boat.

PROVERBS 3:9

Honor the LORD with your wealth.

FISHERMEN HAVE REACHED THE POINT where the price of fishing lures doesn't seem to matter. As long as we believe we have a good chance to catch a fish, we'll gladly fork out the big bucks for a hot new lure. Even minnows and red worms now can cost $2 or $3 per dozen. It's good that we have titanium split rings (LureSavers) that release the hook and allow us to get our high-dollar plugs back.

†ip

There is generally a tremendous amount of food and forage on rip-raps.

We gladly pay hard-earned dollars for fish bait, but only a small percent of Christians tithe. We could list a log of reasons, but the fact remains when we fail to tithe, we are showing dishonor to the very God who gave us the money in the first place. Truth is, when we honor God He will honor us even more.

LUKE 4:13

After the devil had tempted Jesus in every way,
he left him to wait until a better time.

THE SOLUNAR TABLES are based on a lunar day
(24 hours 50 minutes) and help give us the major
and minor feeding periods for fish and wildlife.
We want to be in our best spots during these feeding
periods. Fishing in the right spot at the right time is
what we're all looking for each time we go out.

Similarly, the devil is always looking for the
right time to cause us problems. Satan's desire is for
terrible things to happen in our life. He also knows
exactly when to attack and tempt us. Maybe
when we're short on money or having family
problems or health problems. Satan will
try to catch us at our weakest moments
and lead us into sin. Your Jesus and
mine has been there. Use His
strength to guide you through
these temptations. Satan will
soon be gone!

†ip

In fairly open water,
turn your trailer hooks
upside down on spinnerbaits
and buzzbaits.

REVELATION 20:15

Anyone whose name was not found written
in the book of life was thrown into the lake of fire.

GROWING UP on the Cleveland County,
Oklahoma, line gave me several
opportunities to fish almost every day.
Lightning Creek ran right behind the
house, and I had three decent size
ponds within bicycle range.
When the preacher began to talk
about hell being a lake of fire,
I visualized those ponds and
Lightning Creek on fire. If Jesus
could keep me out of hell and the
lake of fire, I needed Jesus. Today,
we see these big pipeline and refinery
explosions. These also might be a close picture of
hell. Personally, I'll never know. I've been saved
from hell by Jesus. He died for you and me and
paid for the sins that would throw us into hell.
My name is in that Book of Life! Is yours?

tip
When you catch
a bass,
refish the spot
with another lure.

PHILEMON 1:6

I pray that the faith you share may make you understand every blessing we have in Christ.

WATCHING FOLKS ON TELEVISION catch fish can often cloud what most fishing trips really are. In a single thirty–minute program, we see fish after fish being caught, and sometimes they're all whoppers. Well, we're actually seeing an all–day trip condensed into sort of a highlight show. Plus, nobody on television shows us the bad days . . . only the great days.

Every day that God has given us is a great one. Every day is filled with more of God's blessings than we can count. Yet we still find ways to dwell on whatever is wrong or might go wrong each day. God is pouring out blessings with every breath we take, yet our hearts overflow with evil. You make the choice: "Poor, pitiful me" or "Wow . . . what an awesome God!"

†ip

When trolling, use a lure that runs the same depth that the baitfish are located.

JOHN 4:14

"The water I give will become a spring of water gushing up inside that person, giving eternal life."

DETERMINING WHAT THE WATER is doing at any given time is one of the keys to fishing success. Is it rising, subsiding, warming, chilling, clearing up, getting muddy? Water is always doing something. Pay close attention to what the water is doing. The more you understand the water, the more fish you will catch.

The Bible calls Jesus "living water." Water that gives eternal life. Water that quenches your thirst forever. This means that Jesus is all we need to have life eternal with God. We don't need good looks, power, fame, or even money. All we need is faith in Jesus. Is your pitcher of faith filled with the living water of Jesus?

tip

Determine your hook size by the diameter of the worm, not the length.

JUNE 11

ROMANS 7:15

I do not do what I want to do, and I do the things I hate.

TO ME, CAROLINA RIG WORM fishing is about as close as you can get to not going fishing at all. It's a tremendous technique and really catches fish. In addition, it's really simple to learn and easy to do. For me it's a little like watching lily pad flowers open.

Paul complains in Romans that he commits sins that he hates. We're probably the most guilty of this in close personal relationships such as our family. We seem to treat those we love the most with the most disrespect, the most anger, and the least compassion and affection. When something goes wrong today, bite your tongue, swallow your pride, and speak words of love and encouragement instead of harsh or ugly words.

tip
Slow a worm
with a 1/8 oz. or
1/16 oz. weight
over grassbeds

2 PETER 1:3

Jesus has the power of God, by which he has given us everything we need to live and to serve God.

HOW MANY FISHING LURES does a person need? I've never heard a definite answer, but I'm pretty sure almost all of us already have enough. Yet we still want more. We still buy more. I guess fishing lures are like just about everything else we have. God has supplied our needs, yet we want more. More money, more success, more kids, more grandkids, more land . . . more this . . . more that. We can all build wish lists a mile long. Instead, how about building a "Thanks, God" list of what we do have. Mine would start with my salvation, my family, my health, and then I could go for pages and without reaching the end of the list. God gives everything and more!

tip

When bass begin schooling on shad use a multi–blade spinnerbait.

JUNE 13

LUKE 6:38

"Give and you will receive. The way you give to others is the way God will give to you."

FISHING PROVIDES WONDERFUL opportunities to share with others. We can share our time, our skills, and our experiences. I believe wholeheartedly the more we give to anything, the more we receive back. This is God's plan. This goes way beyond tangible things. It includes attitudes and feelings. The more love we give, the more we'll be loved. Do you want to be happy . . . then give happiness to others. It's amazing how even a simple smile will cause folks to smile back. Those are gifts from God. This deal of God's works both ways. If we give bitterness, anger, harsh words, lies, or anything else bad or negative, that's exactly what we'll receive back.

† i p

For suspended deep water bass, try a float-n-fly technique.

1 TIMOTHY 1:16
*Christ Jesus could show that he has
patience without limit.*

A FLOAT TRIP DOWN one of America's rivers or
streams is a wonderful experience in late spring or
early summer. God has filled the woods to their
fullest of green, and the power of God's presence
seems to be in that moving water. The next time
you have an opportunity to experience this kind of
fishing, consider your salvation. Think about the
day God saved you and became King of your life.
If you have any doubts about whether or not you're
actually saved, that's okay. Maybe God has been
patiently waiting for this moment for you to
come to Him. God's saving power is
certain, and He wants to make sure
you know you've received it!

tip

Live frogs are
excellent for all
species of
freshwater fish—
especially big catfish.

COLOSSIANS 1:13

God has freed us from the power of darkness
and he brought us into the kingdom of his dear Son.

BASS FEED AT NIGHT. In fact, many really big bass
become all but impossible to catch during daylight
hours. Although darkness is our friend when it
comes to fishing, God equates darkness with Satan
and his fallen angel demons. God has even allowed
Satan to have an awesome worldly power on earth.
The devil's power may be greater now in the
United States of America than at any other time.
If you're saved as a Christian who can claim Jesus
as your Lord, you're set apart and no longer held
captive to the devil's power. Satan will still cause
problems, but Jesus will never let
these destroy you. Instead, God will
use these difficulties to strengthen you.

†ip

Really big poppers
catch few fish other
than really big bass—
try the Cordell
Pencil Popper.

Pride leads only to shame; it is wise to be humble.

TOURNAMENT BASS FISHING will humble any
fisherman. The very nature of the game invites
failure. Talk about baseball being a poor percentage
game—get three hits for every ten times at bat and
make the Hall of Fame. How many casts does it
take to catch three bass? I'd take three out of a
hundred every day. We often equate humility with
weakness and failure, but God says humility is a
good thing that produces wisdom. How can that
be? I believe it changes our perspective.
It forces us to look at and rely more
on God and less on ourselves.

So many times, I simply reach
the end of the day and have run
out of solutions, but God has
always been faithful to see
me through.

†ip

Try a scum–frog
beneath trees and
around hard cover during
the summertime.

Catch of the Day   177

JUNE 17

PROVERBS 28:22

Selfish people are in a hurry to get rich
and do not realize they soon will be poor.

SOMETIMES A BASS WILL GRAB your bait and swim off at warp speed. That's a great indication of more bass in that spot. You might have just found a real honey hole. Bass are selfish. They have no desire to share their food. A momma bass won't even share with her own babies.

God warns often about our selfish desires to store up worldly riches.

I, personally, try to mask that desire by calling it *security;* I'm storing up for the bad times that may come. But God wants you and me to share what we have with others and with Him. Sharing is Christ–like; selfishness is devilkin. The frightening part is when we realize that selfishness will drive us to poverty.

tip

Windy days will blow grasshoppers into the water. A Rebel Crickhopper will imitate the real thing.

REVELATION 21:4

*"He will wipe away every tear from their eyes;
there will be no more death, sadness, crying, or pain."*

FISH FEEL NO PAIN. Contrary to what the
anti–fishing folks proclaim, those hooks don't
hurt the fish at all. We, on the other hand,
feel pain in so many ways . . . physically,
spiritually, emotionally. We have lots
of ways to hurt, and it will always
be that way here on earth. Here at
our tiny company, our team
experienced four deaths in four
days running. At such times of
sorrow, we are forced to keep our
eyes and hearts and minds focused
on Jesus. Remember that God has
promised a city of no pain, no crying,
no sickness of any kind, and no death. God calls it
Heaven. It's reserved for you, me, and for everyone
who calls upon Jesus to be saved. It's also more
incredible than we can imagine, but oh what joy
to try!

†ip
Use a fishing log
to remember details
and make you
a better fisherman.

JUNE 19

1 CORINTHIANS 10:13

*You can trust God, who will not permit you
to be tempted more than you can stand. . . .
He will also give you a way to escape.*

ANOTHER JIMMY HOUSTON rule of thumb: find
the heaviest cover near deep water. The heavy cover
gives a bass a great ambush point toward forage, not
a place to hide. The deep water provides an escape
when they're startled or in danger.

Trusting Jesus will not make you immune from
temptation. In fact, it makes you a target, and Satan
may work on you even harder with even
greater temptations. But when you
feed on God's word and then seek
safety in the depths of your faith
in God, He will defend you.
Prayer is another great weapon
we have to fight through
temptation. All too often, my
problem is enjoying these little
temptations. The danger is they're
just like a small seed of sin that has a
great ability to grow. Don't let them start.

tip

Take time
to invite an
old friend fishing.

JOB 42:10

After Job had prayed for his friends,
the LORD gave him success again.

IN THE 1970S we fished a BASS national
tournament on Cherokee Lake in
Tennessee. Cherokee was an incredibly
difficult lake. There wasn't much cover,
the water was clear, and the bass
population was pretty thin. I fished
against a local man named Cecil.
He did pretty well in the
tournament, and his first day's
partner caught the big bass of the
tournament on Cecil's water.
Cecil and I didn't meet in that
tournament, but he remembered me
and followed us on television for years.
I recently visited Cecil in Jonesville, Tennessee.
He has emphysema now and is mostly bedridden.
As I kneeled by his bed, held his hand, and prayed
with him, I was overcome by how much God
loves and cares for each one of His children.

tip

Never give up.
Many tournaments
are won in
the last hour.

HOSEA 6:1

"Come, let's go back to the LORD."

DURING A PRACTICE DAY for a BASS tournament in New Orleans, Chris and I fished several hundred yards of cypress trees. It should have been a dynamite spot, but I only caught one three–pound bass on a Cordell Hot Spot. I didn't return to the area until the last twenty minutes of the tournament. I had a limit, but I needed one decent kicker fish. I didn't catch that exact fish, but I did catch one that was close to three pounds and that helped almost as much.

You don't always find the bass we go back for, but Jesus is always waiting when you return to Him. No matter how far you've drifted, Jesus is still right there. Call on Him now . . . He's waiting.

tip

Try moving to larger hooks with LureSaver split rings on your crankbaits.

MATTHEW 22:39

"'Love your neighbor as you love yourself'."

IF YOU HAVE THE OPPORTUNITY to fish a good smallmouth lake, never underestimate a spinnerbait. Even in the summer. Those brown fish really love brightly colored blades. Solid chartreuse, solid white, or any combination of the same work best. You can tip any of those blades with fluorescent red, and it will really help.

Love also shines brightly and attracts others. Jesus commands us to love others as we love ourselves. What He's really telling us is to take care of the needs of others just like we would take care of our own needs. This is showing love, not merely talking love. Reach out to fill the needs of a neighbor today. Remember, your neighbor just might need Jesus, and you could be the perfect person to fill that need.

✝ip

A crankbait or jerkbait can be used in a Carolina rig instead of soft plastic.

1 THESSALONIANS 4:17

And we will be with the Lord forever.

CLOSE YOUR EYES.

Think of the best fishing water you've ever fished. Now, think about the very best day fishing you've ever had. Put those two together and remember what made that place and that day so special. Multiply that experience in your mind a few thousand times, and you might be just beginning to see what Heaven is like and what being with Lord is all about.

Remember that being with the Lord forever begins the day we're saved, not the day we die. Walking with Jesus every day is a journey you don't want to miss. I wouldn't miss that fishing trip for anything in the world.

† i p
Look for flats
that have
scattered stumps
near deep water.

1 PETER 2:1

So then, rid yourselves of all evil, all lying,
hypocrisy, jealousy, and evil speech.

A PERFECT DAY'S FISHING is hard to come
by, but that's what we're looking for, aren't
we? That day when both the weather and
the fish really cooperate. Not much
wind, not too hot, not too cold,
and a biting fish in just about
every good–looking spot.

Living a perfect life is even
more difficult. Perfection,
however, is what God wants from
us and for us. How do we do that?
By asking Jesus to save us, to
transform us from what we are to what
God wants us to be. Will we instantly become
perfect? No, but our past becomes perfect, and our
future will be aided by God's Holy Spirit.
We'll strive to be perfect with His help, and then
one day, with the help of Jesus, we'll get there.

† i p
Bridge pilings
will hold bass and
crappie mostly
all summer

JUNE 25

TITUS 3:1, 2

Be ready to do good, to speak no evil about anyone,
to live in peace, and to be gentle and polite to all people.

SUMMERTIME FISH ARE SCHOOL FISH. If you can locate one or two, you've probably located a bunch. One of my biggest problems is slowing down enough to really work on the school. I've a bad habit of catching a couple and moving on, only to come back an hour or so later when I can't get a bite anywhere else. I am getting a little better at slowing down and catching a few extra bass. People are a lot like a school of bass; we're generally around a bunch of other folk. It's a busy school we live in, though, and almost too fast–paced to be gentle and polite. If we will make just two words—"thank you"—the most–used words in our vocabulary, then we'll have a positive effect on everyone around us.

tip

Lightning can strike two or three miles in front of the actual storm.

HAGGAI 1:5

*This is what the LORD All–Powerful says:
"Think about what you have done."*

KEEPING A LOG CAN BE BENEFICIAL to most
fishermen. It's particularly helpful if you fish several
different bodies of water. I like to record the
weather, water conditions, dates, and information
on each fish caught. As time goes by, it's amazing
how much you learn by reviewing previous trips.

Most of us are so busy nowadays, we hardly
ever examine ourselves. Over time, we can become
entirely different people. Tiny changes build up
over time like interest on a loan. A little more
complaining, a little more gossip, envy, pride,
hatefulness. A little more negativity.
You get the picture. Take a hard look
at who you are today . . . every
attitude, every feeling. What do
you see?

tip

Fence rows
to a bass are like
steak bones
to a dog.

EZEKIEL 16:49

"'This was the sin of your sister Sodom: she and her daughter were proud and had plenty of food and lived in great comfort, but she did not help the poor and needy'."

I'VE HEARD IT A MILLION TIMES . . . oh, what big, fat, beautiful bass! We like our bass fat and our women skinny. Half of America is on some sort of diet. We live in the most abundant country the world has ever known. With that has come the most pride in the history of mankind. Pride so big it threatens America's very existence. From gay pride to the sociopolitical pride that kicks God out of government, and even our homes, many people have become too proud to be saved by God. God destroyed Sodom because her pride and great comfort reached the heavens. How high is the pride of Americans piled before Almighty God—and how long will He wait?

† í ρ

Willowleaf blades
work best
when fishing grass.

2 PETER 3:8

To the Lord one day is as a thousand years,
and a thousand years is as one day.

MY BUDDY HANK PARKER once told me that what happens today won't matter a thousand years from now. He is right, and I guess if we all took on every day with that attitude we'd be a lot better off. God probably doesn't wear a watch or even own a calendar. The Bible says He never sleeps, so an alarm clock wouldn't be of much use to Him. Our whole lives here on this earth are just a sigh or just a breath. This lifetime is just a speck in the grand scheme of time. What does matter is that a thousand years from now we'll be alive in either Heaven or hell. That's why God doesn't sleep. He's busy raising up preachers, Sunday School teachers, missionaries, singers, musicians, laypeople, your friends, and even you to tell about the Good News of Jesus.

†ip

With a
jig or worm,
most strikes are on
the fall or drop.

JUNE 29

HEBREWS 10:24

*Let us think about each other and help each other
to show love and do good deeds.*

THERE IS AN OLD JOKE about hole–jumpers in
tournament fishing—*I guess they thought I needed
help on that spot so they crowded in and helped me
fish it.* Obviously, this doesn't help; it hurts
fishermen and it's not at all what God is talking
about in today's scripture. Jesus said that loving
and helping others is just about as important
as loving God. Why? Because God's whole
being is about love and about help.
He created Adam and Eve with His
love and helped them daily.
All through the Bible this
picture is revealed over and
over, especially in the life,
death, and resurrection of Jesus
being the ultimate expression of
God's love and help. Loving and
helping others might be just the
very best ways to make God smile.

†ip
If the fish are schooling,
have several rods
rigged with lures that
they might bite.

PSALM 33:11

But the LORD's plans will stand forever;
his ideas will last from now on.

AT THE BASS CLASSIC in Charlotte, North
Carolina, in 2004, I ran into a longtime good
friend I hadn't seen in a few years—Jon Hall.
Jon was an excellent tournament
fisherman for many years, but he
hasn't competed in a while.
Jon told me he has terminal
cancer and had come to the
Classic to visit with as many of
his old friends as he could. It was
so good to see him, and it meant
a great deal to me that he came by
to visit. I may never see him again this
side of Heaven.

As we grow older, we see more and more of
our friends go through these types of problems.
We are all appointed by God a day to leave this
earth. Praise God that He's already prepared a
better place for us to spend forever!

tip

A small sponge
on your jig hook
can help hold
fish attractant scent.

July

JULY 1

1 KINGS 3:12, 13

I will do what you asked. I will give you wisdom and understanding. I will also give you what you did not ask for; riches and honor.

SOME OF THE BETTER DAYS I've had crappie fishing were days when I actually was bass fishing. Sometime during the day, I'd catch a crappie on a bass lure, pick up a Road Runner, and proceed to catch a livewell full of big slabs. What I'd intended (catching bass) didn't work out too well, but success was supplied in another way (catching crappie). That happens a lot in life, too.

When we pray, God tells us in advance what He wants us to pray for in order to have successful prayers and spiritual life. He tells us what He wants to hear! All too often I'm only interested in my needs and intentions, not God's desires. He knows our needs and is ready and able to supply them. What God wants is our hearts.

tip

Locate bass with fast-moving crankbaits.

JUDE 24

God is strong and can help you not to fall.

GUS RHOTON IS 95 years old. I took him fishing
one summer. The lake was high, and for us to get to
the dock, we had to walk a warped two–by–twelve
plank for about ten feet. When he saw it, he simply
said, "No," emphatically about three or four times.
Finally the rest of us assured him we would wade in
the water along both sides and would
not let him fall. He walked the plank,
got in the boat, and caught several
nice bass. Gus told us he didn't get
to be 95 by being stupid.

    We don't need to be stupid
about God. He is able to hold us
in safety, no matter what the
circumstances or how high the
water. When we really trust Him
completely, God will not let us fall.

tip
Share a day
of fishing with
a senior citizen.
The blessing
will be yours.

JULY 3

REVELATION 3:20

"Here I am; I stand at the door and knock."

IT CAN BE ALL but impossible sometimes to find fish. We've all been there. Sometimes we just run out of options and have no idea where to look next. Without help, those days usually end in total failure. But with just a little tip or two from a friend we can completely turn that day around.

When we run out of options with a problem in everyday life, Jesus is that friend with the solution. No matter how much we have failed in any situation, Jesus can turn it into success. Amazingly, He is always standing there, ready to help . . . ready to give that victory. He's knocking on the door of our hearts. We just need to open up to Him!

†ip

Peg your slip sinker in heavy vegetation

ROMANS 12:21

Do not let evil defeat you, but defeat evil by doing good.

THE DROP SHOT TECHNIQUE can be dynamite in
the hot summer; almost everything about it is
advantageous. Just using light line gives us a little
help. With the weight on the bottom and hook tied
above the weight, we can really put a lot of action
on these tiny, soft plastic baits. The smallness of
the lure also is a distinct advantage.

Pretty much all aspects of doing good
also are positive, but the devil hates when we
do it. With so much evil in the world, it's
great to know we can defeat evil with good.
When we're exhausted and put down by
others, our weapon is to pray for them
to do good to them. Evil will be
the loser.

†ip

Bumping a
stump or log with
your spinnerbait often
produces a strike.

JULY 5

2 PETER 2:9

The Lord knows how to save those who serve him when troubles come.

HEAVY RAINS DURING the summer are rare, but when they happen, they completely change how we go about catching bass. Most summertime bass spend the daylight hours down in deeper water. Heavy rains and rising water will drive these fish to the bank. This is particularly true up in the river areas of a lake. These fish don't have far to go and can get there really quick when that "new water" starts pouring in. Unlike the heavy summer rains which are rare, troubles will come even to those who serve God. At times, it seems unfair to do God's work and still have problems but we do. We must remember that we serve a God who has the power to rescue us from whatever trouble we get ourselves into. For me, I certainly do need lots of God's help.

tip
An undersized worm hook will cost you missed strikes and lost bass.

JULY 6

DEUTERONOMY 26:18

The LORD has said you are his very own people. But you must obey his commands.

IT'S IMPORTANT TO BE a member of something—a bass club, BASS, FLW, the Federation—we all want to belong and be a part of something special. God has called us out as Christians to be His very own. We're set apart to be different than the rest of the world who can't call Jesus the King and Lord of their lives. We're actually members of God's family. Our requirement is to obey Him at all times. Almost all of Christianity can be summed up as *obey God.* This is the single most important element of our relationship with God once we are saved. We obey God for His satisfaction and for our good. Rest assured, God wants only the best for you and me.

†ip

A noisy bait, like a Cordell Hot Spot, will locate suspended smallmouth.

JULY 7

EPHESIANS 3:20

With God's power working in us, God can do much,
much more than anything we can ask or imagine.

IT IS SO FRUSTRATING to not be able to find fish
or figure out how to catch them. It is doubly so for
those who know a great deal about the game.
Quite often, just a little clue from nature or the
environment can unlock the problem.
Cloud cover, wind, a bass swirling
on baitfish, or shad flickering on
top can end the frustration if we
can put all the variables together.
When we have God in us and
working for us, He will
accomplish so much more on
our behalf. We have a God who
will always go the extra mile.
He will always strengthen and
encourage us just a little bit more.
We have a God who sets our goals for us much
higher than we set them for ourselves.

† i ρ
Let your
worms and tubes fall
on slack line.

ISAIAH 26:7

The path of life is level for those who are right with God.

WINDY DAYS IN JULY and August are a blessing in the South. In fact, if we can just get a little breeze in the "dog days" of summer it really makes a difference. Most of the year, though, wind and good fishing don't go hand in hand. We like nice level water. God says that if you get right with Him, your path through life will be smooth. Does that mean we'll have no problems, no bumps, no mountains? Of course not! Very few people, if any, will go through life like that. I believe what that promise means is that God will smooth out those bumps and mountains. Reliance on Him and knowing with confidence that He holds my future can flatten even the roughest terrain!

tip
A rubber frog bait is ideal for heavy vegetation in ponds and lakes.

HABAKKUK 3:2

Even when you are angry, remember to be kind.

CHRIS HAS ALWAYS SAID, "If Jimmy is mad, ask him for his autograph; he treats nicely everyone who he meets." Her observation is humorous, but it has given me some serious food for thought. As usual, she's right. No matter how upset, no matter what my problems, no matter what the situation . . . I can smile and be nice to a total stranger while at the same time being "Mr. Grumpy" to someone I loved. God knows things at times will upset us. Even Jesus became angry. God becomes angry.

But God wants us to pause and be kind even when situations upset us. Praise God that He's still kind even when we anger Him!

† i p

A hard bottom generally will show up as a double or triple echo on your locator.

JOHN 20:31

These are written so that you may believe
that Jesus is the Christ, the Son of God.

STRUCTURE FISHING IS ONE of the keys to summertime bass fishing success. Finding a channel edge, a hump, or a secluded deep–water brush pile can be a real bonanza. Trusting your depth finder is a must. Most of us don't really know how these units work or how those tiny little chips inside can give us so much information. Somehow we have faith that what we see is actually a roadbed, bridge, drop off, school of shad, and so on.

Tip

Learn to determine the pattern within a pattern.

Like a depth finder, God gave man His Word to show us that Jesus is indeed the Christ, the Messiah, the powerful and almighty King. God's desire is that we all come to Him through His blessed Son to be saved.

JULY 11

ROMANS 8:31
If God is with us, no one can defeat us.

DURING OUR OKLAHOMA SOONER Caravan Bass
Tournament on Lake Tenkiller, coaches and players
fish with selected local bass anglers in the celebrity
competition. Many want to draw me as their
partner, because they think they can't lose with me.
Of course that's not true, but one year I fished with
the athletic director, Joe Castiglione, and defensive
back Matt McCoy. Joe and I won the tournament
by barely edging out Matt's team, and I
received plaques for both first and
second places.

With God on your team
you'll achieve victory every time.
No matter what or who is your
adversary, the ultimate victory
lies with God. Team up today.

+ip
The hotter
the weather,
the slower I fish a
topwater bait.

2 TIMOTHY 3:16

All Scripture is given by God and is useful for teaching, for showing people what is wrong in their lives, for correcting faults, and for teaching people how to live right.

If you could get your hands on the ultimate fish–catching book, what would it be worth to you? Every tip, every trick, every idea and technique ever developed. Guaranteed success every time out on the water.

How about a book that tells you everything you need to know about every situation and encounter in your life? This book is available and was written by the almighty God who hung the moon and stars. He cares for you and me so much that He gave us a handbook to live by. Your marriage, health, family, job, hobbies, relationships, worship, attitudes, even your money . . . the answers are all in there and more. God created us, and He wants only the very best for all aspects of our lives.

tip

Stained water farm ponds offer great summertime fishin'.

JULY 13

PSALM 121:3

He who guards you never sleeps.

AT A YOUTH FISHING DAY in South Bend, Indiana,
I walked along the shore and visited with the four
hundred or five hundred kids fishing. We came
upon a little girl lying down, half asleep as her
bobber went under. "Wake up, wake up . . . you've
got a fish!" She jumped up, and missed the fish of
course. I told her there's no sleeping in fishing.

We all fall asleep when we shouldn't, but isn't
it comforting to know we have a God who does
not sleep. He's on the job at all times. When
problems mount and worries soar and you find it
impossible to sleep, give everything over to
God. He is going to stay
awake to guard and solve your
problems; there's no need for both
of you to stay up.

tip

If crawfish
are available,
fish shallow.

JAMES 4:10

Don't be too proud in the Lord's presence,
and he will make you great.

JUST ABOUT EVERY FISHERMAN has an ego, and
we really enjoy it when someone strokes that ego.
If no one does, we will do it ourselves. We do this
particularly if we are around someone who we
believe has more than us or who might be better
than us. Of course we all really want
to be something special and great,
but God tells us simply to be
humble in His presence. You see,
we can fool the world, but we
cannot fool God. He always
knows! He knows how pride can
hurt us. He knows what a trap it
is. He knows what it will cost us
and what mistakes it will cause us to
make. He knows all, and He sure
enough knows how to reward the humble.
That's a promise.

tip

Tungsten slip-sinkers
penetrate grass better than
lead weights do.

JULY 15

LUKE 15:10

"There is joy in the presence of the angels of God when one sinner changes his heart and life."

DURING THE TWENTY-ONE YEARS of Bass'n Gal, it was exciting to watch the progress of many of the girls. Some barely stood a chance of catching fish those early days, but they became excellent fisherpersons over the course of time. Their fish-catching ability changed right before our eyes.

When you get saved, God gets excited about seeing changes happen in every aspect of your life, perhaps most importantly in your heart. Your ole sinful, sin-loving heart is washed clean. All sins are forgotten and a new you begins to develop. When you really, really turn it over to God, He will turn your life into a brand new exciting adventure.

†ip

A red crankbait will produce in stained water really well.

EPHESIANS 5:21

Yield to obey each other because you respect Christ.

IT'S NO SECRET that my best fishing partner is my beautiful wife, Chris. I've spent literally thousands of hours with her in a boat and am still just as excited about the hours we'll spend fishing together tomorrow. I can't imagine what it would be like to have a non–Christian wife. I know she wouldn't live with a non–Christian husband.

When people make a commitment to love, cherish, honor, and obey, it's pretty easy to skim over that "obey" part. I'm not sure it would be possible without mutually yielding to obey. And this is a gift from God. The devil hates this kind of godly marriage. He really deplores our respect of Jesus Christ. Bottom line . . . I guess it's godly to carry out the trash when she asks you to!

tip

If you hear thunder within thirty seconds of a lightning strike— seek cover.

JULY 17

PSALM 85:8

I will listen to God the LORD.

AS GOOD AS FISHING is in the springtime, it's hard
for me to totally concentrate on catching fish. Why?
Because I'm always listening for a turkey gobble.
Most of the time I keep camo attire and a shotgun
in the boat. Even if it happens during tournament
practice, when a turkey gobbles I'm
outta there! Into the woods!

It pays to listen just as intently
for a word from God. I believe
God has the power to
communicate with us daily . . .
even hourly . . . if we'll but
listen. He has all the answers,
so why not pay attention every
minute of every day? It doesn't
make much sense to "go it alone" in
even the most trivial matters, let alone
life's major struggles. Make it a priority to listen
to God today.

†ip

A color fish locator
will make it easier
to determine
bottom makeup.

1 JOHN 2:15

Do not love the world or the things in the world.

WE HAVE THE BEST FISHING in the world here in America, Canada, and Mexico. We are also free to travel between these countries to enjoy that fishing. We are particularly blessed here in the United States with an abundance of just about everything. Does God want us to enjoy these things? Absolutely! After all, He created all this for mankind to use and have dominion over. What He does require is for us to love Him and never put the world or worldly things above Him. He created this world and all that is in it for our benefit and our pleasure. He created us for His pleasure. We must always keep God first and never, ever put His creation above the Creator.

†ip

Insert a piece
of nail into a sinking worm
to make it easier
to throw in the wind.

JULY 19

MATTHEW 28:20

"Teach them to obey everything I have taught you and I will be with you always, even until the end of this age."

I REMEMBER MY SON, Jamie, and my dad following us out onto Lake Ontario in huge waves. Jamie was driving my Ranger boat, even though he was only ten or eleven years old. The waves would almost overwhelm the boat, but Jamie was confident and felt secure. Granddad was beside him, and I was in front of him watching for any trouble. There was really nothing for him to fear.

Those who are saved by the blood of Jesus Christ have a Father who will always be there no matter what, even when the storm gets wild and scary. When those we trust fail us, when the devil attacks us . . . count on Jesus. He'll be right there! Always.

†ip

Use a soft plastic jerkbait when bluegill are present in shallow water.

MATTHEW 10:39

*"Those who try to hold on to their lives
will give up true life."*

CATFISH ARE INCREDIBLE. They're really a lot of
fun to catch and tremendous to eat. The amazing
thing to me about catfish is how well they can live
out of water. They somehow can hold on for hours
and still be just fine when pretty much any other
fish would be long gone. When Jesus talks about
holding on to our lives, He's not talking about
breathing. He means clinging to the old sinful
life we lived before we met Him. Take a
little inventory of the ways you are
not Christ–like. Anger, greed,
lying, stealing, bad attitude, not
tithing, pornography, sexual sin
. . . the list could go on and on,
but you get the picture. Now,
start cleaning house.

†ip

Baitfish move
around more
at night.

ACTS 10:43

"All who believe in Jesus will be forgiven of their sins through Jesus' name."

ONE OF THE GREAT THINGS about fishing the Bassmasters Classic is everyone gets a check. We all get paid. We don't have to do anything but qualify for the Classic. We can zero the entire tournament, which some people have done, and still make some pretty good money for the week.

God is an all–inclusive God. He wants no one to go to hell. His desire is that all be saved. He's laid the groundwork for this from the beginning of time. He promised His Son, Jesus, to pay for our sins. How do we qualify for this? Believe in Jesus, whom He sent just like He prophesized for hundreds of years. And here is God's promised paycheck: all sins will be forgiven no matter how many, no matter how terrible, no matter how much trouble they caused. What a God!

†ip

Try jerking a tube or swimming it for smallmouth bass.

DANIEL 1:17

God gave these four young men wisdom and the ability to learn many things that people had written and studied.

Some fishermen have extraordinary ability, while others struggle to catch fish no matter how hard they work at it. Anyone can become better at anything if they work hard, but achieving the top level takes more effort. Quite honestly, it's a gift from God. I can't sing . . . I have a lousy voice. I can't dunk a basketball . . . either I am too short or the goal's too high. I can't do brain surgery . . . I'm not very smart in that area. But there are many, many things that I can do very well. Why? God's gift to me! God has given each of us some very special talents and abilities. I believe He wants us to use these in the very best ways we can, and He prefers we use our gifts for Him! He probably also wants us to be satisfied with what He's given us.

†ip

Beaver huts extend several feet out under the water.

1 CORINTHIANS 15:33

Do not be fooled: "Bad friends will ruin good habits."

MOST OF THE TOURNAMENT GUYS have one or two friends with whom they become really tight. They travel together, eat together, room together, and either practice together or at least share information. I've seen both sides of the coin where this can either help or hurt an individual's chances. Close friendships like this also happen in other activities and aspects of our life.

God doesn't give much leeway here—He pretty much tells us to avoid having bad friends. None of us wants bad friends, but most of us have some who wouldn't rank too high on most folks list. I've had enough to know that you will pay a very high price for poorly chosen relationships nearly every time. God says they will change us for the worse even while He is changing us for the better.

tip

Search out laydown logs that have a fork in the limbs.

EZEKIEL 7:3

"I will judge you for the way you have lived, and I will make you pay for all your actions that I hate."

MOST BASS FISHERMEN DREAD cold fronts, but a cold front in the summertime usually can make it easier to catch fish. We had a cold front in Oklahoma one summer that dropped the temperatures from 92 to 82 degrees. That ten–degree drop, the cause, gave us the effect of the best shallow–water bass fishing since the middle of that spring.

Violating God's laws starts a cause–and–effect cycle that will always carry serious consequences. In today's fast–paced, loose–living society, most of what God hates is becoming standard behavior. Lying, cheating, stealing, adultery, blaming others, and doing other such things has become blended into so many lives. Rest assured, no one is getting away with it even though it appears that they are! God is still God, and He knows it.

†ip

A bass often hears a spinnerbait or crankbait before he sees it.

ISAIAH 29:18

At that time, the deaf will hear . . . the blind will see.

UNDERWATER ROCK PILES are some of the hottest bass–holding structures you can find. Once summertime hits, you can bet bass will start heading for those rocks. A great technique is a heavy roller jig that you can bounce off the rock pile. This extra noise really helps the fish hone in on your bait.

As we get older, our ability to hear and see begins to weaken. Isn't it comforting to know that this regression is only temporary and will change in an instant when we die and move on to our eternal reward with Jesus. As this old body and these old senses wear out, God has already designed a heavenly body—a perfect body. Not only for those of us who have used up this body, but for many who will see and hear for the very first time!

†ip

Always check to make sure your crankbait is running straight.

ROMANS 8:35

Can anything separate us from the love Christ has for us?

BASS USUALLY SCHOOL in most lakes in late summer and early fall. It's terrific and fast–paced fishing. Get a good lure into the school, and it's a fish almost every cast. The problem is they don't stay up long. When they go down it's a waiting game until they resurface. You can always count on a few bass getting separated each time they come up. I usually slow roll a spinnerbait or change to a deep–diving crankbait to pick up a few of these stragglers who've been left behind.

tip
Avoid the heavy summertime traffic by fishing at night.

    We can never be left behind from the love of Jesus. When Jesus stretched out His arms on that cross, He embraced you and me with a love that can't be shaken. Nothing Satan or his legion of demons can do or lead us into can dampen Christ's love. Trust Jesus—He'll prove it every day.

JULY 27

ZEPHANIAH 2:7

The LORD their God will pay attention to them and will make their life good again.

It is frustrating to go those stretches when you can't get a bite. If you fish tournaments, those stretches can quickly turn into the entire day, then two days, then several tournaments. Life, relationships, and business seem to throw these stretches at us also. The devil has a way of jumping in here and piling on. One problem leads to another. Troubles seem to come in bunches and from all directions. It looks like there's no way out. That's when we need God most, and that's when God is at His best. That is when we don't *need* to pray, we *have* to pray. We don't just read God's Word, we immerse ourselves in it and live in it. I have seen God walk on water many times, and I'm counting on Him to do it again.

†ip

In general,
fish a buzzbait as slowly
as possible.

JULY 28

1 PETER 5:8

Control yourselves and be careful! The devil, your enemy, goes around like a roaring lion, looking for someone to eat.

YOU'LL CATCH MORE FISH on windy days if you'll use baits you can control in the wind. Baits like Hot Spots, Zara Spooks, tungsten spinnerbaits, a tube, or a jig. Those baits cut into the wind. Baits that we can't control create lots of problems.

Not being able to control what we say, do, and think is gunpowder in the devil's barrel. We have so much to guard! We must be very careful with our attitudes, our feelings, and our desires. When you feel yourself losing it, pause and ask yourself who you belong to. If you belong to God, ask Him to come in and take charge. When I give God control of the situation I have no doubt He will do a much better job with it than I could ever do.

† i p

Create your own holes in heavy vegetation to fish later in the day.

REVELATION 14:7

"Fear God and give him praise, because the time has come for God to judge all people."

BOAT DOCKS ARE PRIME for summertime fishing. Bass, bluegill, crappie, catfish . . . they're all there. Naturally, you can make any dock better by adding a fish feeder, but it also helps to add brush. Cedar or Christmas trees work well, but it's better to use hardwoods because they last longer and are easier to fish. Don't be afraid to hang up in the brush; a few lost lures will be worth the fish you'll catch.

Why should we be afraid of God? He is a loving God, a caring God, a forgiving God. He's also a Holy God and will accept nothing less than holiness from those He created in His own image. Can we become holy? Sure—we become holy by trusting Jesus and partaking in His perfection. With the Lord Jesus, we have nothing to fear and nothing to lose that's worth missing out on Him.

†ip

As bass become inactive, switch to a smaller spinnerbait.

ROMANS 8:37

But in all these things, we have full victory through God
who showed his love for us.

MY DECISION NOT TO WEAR a beer patch or place
a beer decal on my boat created some costly
problems over the years. Although I lost that battle,
maybe I won the war. Now no angler is required to
promote beer. It is an option.

Nothing we encounter in life can defeat us if
we are saved and belong to Jesus. The full victory we
have is eternal life with God. No sickness, no bad
relationship, no amount of lost money,
no heartbreak, not even death can take
this ultimate victory away. God is a
mighty, loving God, and He showed
us His love in a mighty way by
sending Jesus to die on that cross
for you and for me.

† i p

Try a white jig
in clear water under
milfoil or
coontail moss.

MATTHEW 11:28

"Come to me, all of you who are tired and have heavy loads, and I will give you rest."

MAKING YOUR BAIT RUN into something is one of the tricks of almost all good fishermen. Letting a spinnerbait, crankbait, jig, worm, or whatever bump a stump, log, or bush doesn't happen by accident. Look for opportunities to create this as much as you can.

Just like good things happen on purpose, it's also no accident when you become weary and seemingly carry the world on your shoulders. The devil is at work every day creating tough situations. Jesus is perfectly capable of handling these trying times.

Quite frequently God has provided the solution in advance. We miss this at times until we become so desperate that we finally realize we have only one place to turn, Jesus. Only then do we realize that God was carrying the load all along.

tip

Use a firetiger crankbait in muddy water.

A.

B.

NAME
THAT LURE

___ Crankbait
___ Hot Spot
___ Jerkbait
___ Jig
___ Road Runner
___ Spinnerbait
___ Topwater
___ Tube
___ Worm

C.

I.

H.

D.

G.

F.

E.

C, I, G, D, A, E, B, H, F

August

AUGUST 1

1 CORINTHIANS 6:12

"I am allowed to do all things," but all things are not good for me to do.

WHEN I WAS A KID working on the dock at Elk Creek on Lake Tenkiller, I always envied the rich kids from the city who seemed to have everything. They had great boats, charged their gas and everything else to daddy's bill, and generally were allowed to do anything they wanted. I saw all this while I worked at a dollar an hour. I also saw a lot of those kids get into all sorts of trouble. Our heavenly Father gives us free will to do all things, but He's also given us His Spirit to guide us and keep us from harming others and ourselves. Pray for His involvement, listen for His guidance, and act upon His advice and leadership.

†ip

Bass normally hang around any commercial docks that sell minnows.

TITUS 3:9

Stay away from those who have foolish arguments

CHRIS'S MOM IS OVER 70 years old (don't tell her I told you this), but she still loves to fish. She still catches her share of bass and catfish, plus more bluegill than anyone. She also loves her God and her church and is there helping, working, and worshiping anytime the doors are open. She knows about everything going on at Keys Baptist Church, and the amazing thing is she won't argue about anything with anybody in that church. Chris says her mom just "plays dumb" when someone wants to create a controversy. Staying out of arguments is probably the smartest thing any church member could do. Let's face it, loving and encouraging each other is honoring God. Arguing and tearing down is honoring Satan. You make the call.

tip
Heavy late afternoon thunderstorms quickly move fish into runoff areas.

AUGUST 3

1 TIMOTHY 6:7
We brought nothing into this world
so we can take nothing out.

ALL TOURNAMENTS START with everyone at zero.
We're not handicapped by a scoring system. We all
have empty livewells. Within minutes after takeoff,
the standings begin to change. We all have the
chance throughout the tournament to win or lose.

We're born into this life with nothing, and
then within seconds we're wrapped in blankets and
we begin to acquire stuff. In the United
States, we have the opportunity to
acquire staggering amounts of
possessions, but at the end of our
lives, we all leave with exactly
what we started with—nothing.
Sure, many people have been
buried with momentos, jewelry,
prized possessions, even money,
but all that stuff remains in that
box as we move on. Where we go
depends not on what we own, but on
who owns us—Jesus or Satan.

tip
When you cull
during a tournament,
mark the next two or three
fish you want to cull.

JEREMIAH 31:3

The LORD appeared to his people and said,
"I love you people with a love that will last forever."

WE'RE FINANCING BOATS now at Jimmy Houston
Marine for ten years or twelve years.
Manufacturers are building boats better
than ever now, but you need to take
care of one pretty good to make it
last that long. The real key is to
start out with the best quality
boat you can buy. The better the
boat, the longer it's likely to last.

†ip

Use Reel Magic
on your dash and
fish locators to keep them
looking new.

God's love for His redeemed
is permanent. The quality of His
love surpasses anything we can
imagine. It's a love I count on every
single day. Just about everyone will let us
down and disappoint us, but not God. We, too,
will at times fail and hurt others, often the people
we love most, but God's command to us is to never
waiver with His love, no matter what.

AUGUST 5

1 PETER 5:10

After you suffer for a short time, God, who gives all grace, will make everything right.

ENJOY EVERY DAY you have fishing. Cherish every moment with your family and friends. Live every day in service to your God. We've lost many fishing friends in the past few years to cancer. We have several who are fighting it now. Sugar Ferris of Bass'n Gal penned these words:

> *Cancer is so limited . . .*
> *It cannot cripple love.*
> *It cannot shatter hope.*
> *It cannot corrode faith.*
> *It cannot eat away peace.*
> *It cannot destroy confidence.*
> *It cannot kill friendship.*
> *It cannot shut out memories*
> *It cannot silence courage*
> *It cannot invade the soul.*
> *It cannot reduce eternal life.*
> *It cannot lessen the power of*
> *   the resurrection.*

Thank you, Sugar Ferris.
Thank You, Jesus!

†ip

Summertime crappie and white bass are active at night using lights under bridges.

PSALM 25:7

Do not remember the sins and
wrong things I did when I was young.

AT PERSONAL APPEARANCES I like to tease moms
and dads with teenagers. I tell them not to worry
about what their sons and daughters will do with
the opposite sex; just remember what they did
when they were their kids' age. Of course, we all
remember how we were less than
perfect and we hope our kids aren't
doing some of the same things we
did as teenagers. The truth is, we
all sin. If I could live my life over
I could write down several pages
of sins I would not commit
again. Nevertheless, those
grievous, foolish, youthful sins
cannot be uncommitted. Praise God
that through His Son, Jesus, they are
forgiven and forgotten by the God who
created us.

tip

A simple change in cloud cover
and sunlight may necessitate
changing lure colors.

AUGUST 7

EPHESIANS 4:2

Always be humble, gentle, and patient,
accepting each other in love.

BETTER FISHERMEN LEARN to adapt to changing conditions. In the South this can happen several times in a single day, while in California, conditions might not change but once every two or three weeks. Rest assured, though, when conditions change you'd better have a few tricks up your sleeve.

One unchanging characteristic of Jesus is accepting us with love, and He expects us to do the same. Jesus expects us to love not just when others love us, but at all times. When we're hurt, we help. When we're lied to, we tell the truth. When we're cheated, we pay back. When we're hurt, we heal. When we're betrayed, we forgive. Is this easy? Absolutely not! But that's what Jesus did for us.

✝ tip

A white blade
is more visible
on a spinnerbait in
murky, muddy water.

AUGUST 8

EPHESIANS 2:10

God made us to do good works, which God planned
in advance for us to live our lives doing.

TODAY'S FISHING REELS are technical works of
art. We've come so far in my lifetime with reels, it's
hard to imagine how they could get any better, but
somehow they will continue to improve. We started
with such a simple concept and have developed to
actually having computers in our fishing reels.
All of this just to make fishing more pleasurable for
you and me.

God is also in the improvement business.
He can take a simple saved sinner and transform
that person into a mountain of
blessing and good to millions.
He's done it time after time
throughout thousands of years.
He saved each individual
Christian to do good works.
Talk to God today about the
good works He has planned for
you to do.

> **tip**
> Remember, crawdads
> are nocturnal,
> they move around
> mostly at night.

1 CORINTHIANS 6:1

When you have something against another Christian, how can you bring yourself to go before judges who are not right with God?

BEING IN THE BOAT BUSINESS and fishing on television seems to put a target square on our backs. We've been sued just trying to help a friend sell his boat. Such are the times in America today. We reach out as far as we can to place the blame on someone else . . . anyone else. It only takes a little nudging from Satan for good people to do bad things.

God, of course, knew this would happen, and He admonished His people to settle their differences among themselves rather than trusting the situations to an ungodly judicial system. Christians will often wrong other Christians. God knew this, and He's prepared to get involved in the solutions if we will let Him. After all, God is the ultimate Judge.

tip

A low stretch line will improve our hookset.

PROVERBS 31:10

It is hard to find a good wife,
because she is worth more than rubies.

MANY A MAN WHO LOVES to fish has a wife who
doesn't. God's gift to me was not only a wife who
loved to fish, but one who is really good at it. Folks
all across the country remind me often that she
catches more fish than me. Thanks, but I've been
aware of that for a long time. If you want your wife
to become your best fishing partner, make sure
she's having fun. Don't kick her out of bed before
daylight to accompany you to a lousy fishing hole
on a cold rainy day. Pick out the most beautiful,
comfortable day you can and don't go early.
Fish the last few hours before sunset.
Go to your very best honey hole, fish
for whatever is biting, and don't
gripe at her, no matter what!
Then, let God do the rest.

†ip

It pays to carry
a prop wrench and
an extra prop.

MATTHEW 5:44

"But I say to you, love your enemies.
Pray for those who hurt you."

WHEN WE WERE BUILDING our house on Twin
Eagle Lake, we encountered more problems than
you could shake a stick at. We faced delays,
misinformation, shortages, and all kinds of troubles.
I developed calluses that became bigger every day.
Many times Chris warned me to forgive anyone
who seemed like they were part of the problems,
but I really didn't want to. Finally, God used Chris's
nudging and convinced me to forgive. When I did,
He quickly asked me to pray for the one who hurt
me. That was difficult, but I did. Divinely,
supernaturally, God healed me and
gave me the peace I didn't have. If
you're harboring bad feelings toward
anyone, pay close attention to Jesus.
Forgive. Pray.

✝ip

Try drop-shotting
on those clear,
color bright sunny days.

PSALM 23:6

Surely your goodness and love will be with me all my life,
and I will live in the house of the LORD forever.

ALL CHRIS AND I NEED is an excuse to go our ranch and lake house. As much as we love beautiful Lake Tenkiller, we love Twin Eagle Ranch even more.

King David's most famous Psalm isn't talking about a mere lake house, a country home, a church, a temple, or a mansion. It's talking about living in the very presence of God Almighty. Can we do that? You bet we can. In every situation, in every temptation, in every crisis, His presence is only a whisper away. We only need to call on God and He's there quicker than a heartbeat. Many times, we've blurted out God's name for help in sudden danger. God is on call constantly. The devil wants to come between us, but he can't if we'll let God's presence surround us at all times.

tip

Small blades
on a larger spinnerbait
allow you
to fish deeper.

AUGUST 13

1 TIMOTHY 6:11

Live in the right way, serve God, have faith, love, patience, and gentleness.

FISHING INVOLVES so many decisions, especially bass fishing. We make hundreds of decisions every time we go fishing. To catch fish, though, we can base all these decisions on only a handful of criteria.

To live our lives correctly, we need to do only a handful of things. We must serve God, have faith, have love, be patient, and be gentle. Can you think of a single time, place, relationship or activity where these five godly characteristics can fail you? Maybe we should write them on our calendars, desks, the dashboards of our cars, or even on our tackle boxes. What if we just started this right way of living within our own families and let it blossom from there? Trust me, God will do some mighty things.

tip
Follow the
morning shade
as long
as you can.

JOHN 9:4

*"While it is daytime, we must continue doing
the work of the One who sent me."*

WITHOUT A DOUBT, fishing is really hard work
when it's done correctly. Very few fishermen can
put in the five or six long days that
tournament guys do every tournament.
It is pretty difficult for most anglers
to fish really hard and really well
throughout the competition.

tip
Don't seek
safety under trees
during a
lightning storm.

God, however, is always on
the ball, whatever the job, and we
need to be working for Him.
Maybe His work can be summed
up in just a couple of powerful
words . . . *love* and *forgive*. Jesus
performed many miracles, preached great
sermons, and changed countless lives. Pretty much
everything Jesus did, including dying on that cross
and rising again, was done to love and to forgive.
God asks for exactly the same for you and me.
We may never walk on water, but we can love
and we can forgive.

AUGUST 15

MATTHEW 7:17

Every good tree produces good fruit,
but a bad tree produces bad fruit.

ANOTHER OF JIMMY'S RULES of thumb—fish the heaviest cover you can find near deep water. Bass get big and mean, but they can be spooked easily. Heavy cover and deep water produce good protection, so that's where you'll most likely find fish.

Matthew isn't talking about factors that make good fishin'; he's warning us about the results of our actions. We must guard what we do. People pay more attention to our actions than our words. They see what we stand for without our telling them. Non–Christians love to see Christians mess up and fail. It's important that our actions match what we say and attract others to Jesus.

тip

Try to determine
how fish are
positioning on
a piece of structure.

ISAIAH 35:2

Everyone will see the glory of the LORD,
and the splendor of our God.

THERE ARE SPECTACULAR PLACES to fish around
the world. Most of Alaska is like fishing in a
picture postcard. There's stunning beauty in just
about any direction. I'm told New Zealand
and Switzerland are just as breathtaking.

But I'm sure none of these compare
to the splendor and glory of the God
who made them. The Bible tells us
our finite minds can't comprehend
God's infinite glory. We also can't
comprehend His love, but we can
experience it. Through Jesus,
God has provided us a ticket into
the most glorious Kingdom ever . . .
Heaven. He has chosen us to be set
apart for this glory . . . this incredible
splendor. I'm not too sure what to expect,
but I wouldn't miss it for the world.

TIP
Be alert
for schooling bass
in late summer and
early fall.

AUGUST 17

1 PETER 5:10

He will make you strong and support you and keep you from falling.

ONE OF THE BEST TECHNIQUES for fishing standing timber is pitching a worm or tube right at the tree and letting it fall. The trick is to use slack line. Move your rod tip toward the tree to keep your line slack. If it's deep, peel off line to keep your bait right on that timber.

By giving us free will, God gives us a lot of slack in making choices, good or bad. Do you know people who never seem to fall or make a bad choice, no matter what? They always seem strong and positive no matter how dark the situation. Their secret is in living near to God.

Sure, there are times when there seems to be no hope . . . God becomes our hope. We run out of strength . . . God is our strength. We have questions . . . God has the answers. He is our support and will keep us from falling.

+ i p

Try a square nose crankbait around brush in dingy water.

MARK 8:36

*"It is worth nothing for them to have
the whole world if they lose their souls."*

WHAT'S YOUR MOST PRIZED fishing possession?
Your Ranger boat, your best Shimano reel, your
boxes full of lures, your fishing trophies and
awards? Think about it. What if you could double
or triple or have a hundred times more of that
prized possession? What kind of price
would you pay, and how much effort
would you put out to get there?
Would you give your soul?
Of course not is what most folks
would answer. Yet, many have
and many more will. We often
fail in setting our priorities. Our
most prized possession is our soul.
It's ours to keep with Jesus or ours
to lose with Satan. It's a choice every
one of us must make. Most folks already have.

tip
Search out
stumps on
the edge of drains.

AUGUST 19

DEUTERONOMY 28:2

*Obey the LORD your God so that all these blessings
will come and stay with you.*

MANY TIMES IN TOURNAMENTS I've just missed
finding a really big bunch of bass. Maybe I was on
a spot at the wrong time, didn't go far enough up a
creek, or didn't go far enough down the bank.
I might have used the wrong lure or technique. I was
close but made mistakes that cost me. Probably
every tournament angler can identify
with this.

I believe that often we come
close to God's blessing but miss
out because of things we do or
don't do. Not thinking robs us
of blessings. Sinning sexually,
being greedy, envying, gossiping,
telling lies, being proud, and
committing other sins short us on
God's blessings. God laid out a very
well–defined path to receive and keep His
blessings. Obey God.

† i p
Feeding periods
generally change
roughly fifty minutes
each day.

LUKE 12:15

Then Jesus said, "Be careful and guard against all kinds of greed. Life is not measured by how much one owns."

CHRIS HAS SAID MANY TIMES that it's sinful how many fishing lures, worms, and spinnerbaits we have. It scares me to think that Jesus just might agree with her. Perhaps even worse, we still keep getting more.

Jesus was never hung up on stuff. He sent His disciples out to preach with almost nothing but His word. He wants us to have a relationship with Him and with the Father. He knows what this life is all about.

Two or three times during our forty years of marriage, Chris and I have come very close to losing everything, and I mean everything. We had accumulated so much stuff, but it was all about to go away. Once we were at peace with losing it all, God stepped in and saved us.

Life is measured by how much God owns us.

†ip

Use large willow leaf blades in water with poor visibility.

JUDGES 21:25

In those days Israel did not have a king. Everyone did what seemed right.

AT ANY GIVEN TIME, on any body of water, you can catch fish in a lot of different ways. Almost any lure or technique will work, but obviously some work much better than others. We all fish in what we believe is the right way with the right bait.

tip

Use fluorocarbon line in super clear water.

Without leadership, people are on their own to determine right and wrong. Without God, what seems to be the right way becomes more perverse, more sinful. Here in America, many things unheard of when I was a kid are now accepted as normal behavior. Some are not only accepted but are openly rewarded. We make light of sexual sin. Lying, cheating, and greed are open parts of business, and employees believe they have a right to steal. At the same time, Christian values are routinely mocked.

Who's leading your sense of right and wrong?

2 THESSALONIANS 2:7

The secret power of evil is already working in the world,
but there is one who is stopping that power.

THERE'VE BEEN MANY SECRET lures and techniques
come along over the years. I won the 1986 BASS
Angler of the Year primarily on a tandem
willowleaf spinnerbait and kept the lure a secret
until the first tournament or two. The drop shot,
gitzit, Road Runner, frog, square nose crankbait,
Carolina rig, and many, many more techniques
were once secrets shared by very few fishermen.

Here's another secret that needs to be made
known: Satan is at work in this world. Some
Christians don't even realize how the devil is
affecting, or even controlling, their
lives. Realize with all certainty—Satan
is real and extremely powerful.
So powerful, he will completely
destroy you without Jesus Christ.

tip

Use a 1/4 ounce
Road Runner head
with a Zoom Fluke Jr.
for finicky bass.

1 TIMOTHY 11:9

Those who want to become rich bring temptation
to themselves and are caught in a trap.

WE GET A LOT OF MAIL here at Jimmy Houston
Outdoors. A few times each week there's a letter
about an idea or invention that the sender claims
will revolutionize fishing and make us all rich.
Although sometimes we do hear about great ideas
and products, most will never make anybody
any money.

Without a doubt, wanting to make more
money is tempting, but God tells us it is definitely
a trap. I've been in that trap many times myself.
Each time, my relationship with God suffered.
Each time, I walked head first into
that trap set by Satan. Each time I
failed. God's simple advice is to seek
Him first. He will provide
everything we need and more.

†ip

When nights
begin to cool,
morning fishing is better
than evening.

JONAH 2:2

When I was in danger,
I called to the LORD and he answered me.

EVERYONE LOVES THE STORY about Jonah and the big fish. As kids, we sang songs about Jonah and wondered what it would be like to be fishbait. But what about Jonah? He wasn't too thrilled. In fact he was downright mad at God about the whole situation. He didn't want to go to Ninevah, he didn't want to preach, he didn't want the people to repent and be saved. He certainly didn't want to be a big topwater plug.

We all get out of the will of God sometimes. We all disobey God. When we do, trouble and problems are sure to follow. When this happens, we have two choices: we can get mad at God or we can call on God for help. Sooner or later, the second choice will become our only option. Better make it sooner.

†ip

Always wear
a life jacket when
the big engine
is running.

JAMES 4:7

So give yourselves completely to God. Stand against the devil, and the devil will run from you.

EVERY FISHING DAY NEEDS to have a plan. We need to think out in advance how we intend to catch fish. Every tournament fisherman spends a great deal of time at this. Most people modify their plans as the day goes on. Some sell out to their strategies, no matter what. If we are really saved, we need to sell out to Jesus all the way. Too many times in too many situations, we turn our backs on God and His principles. When we do, the devil is right there to inflict pain and suffering. Only when we remain totally in our God can we send the devil packing.

Today, don't play any games with God. Give Him all you've got of yourself and stand back and see what He can do with you!

†ip

Late summer, afternoon thunderstorms can produce some great buzz–bait fishing.

AUGUST 26

1 THESSALONIANS 5:2

*You know very well that the day the Lord comes again
will be a surprise, like a thief that comes in the night.*

SURPRISES CAN BE GOOD or bad. We all enjoy
the surprise of an unexpected top–water
blow–up. We hate the surprise of that
big fish coming unbuttoned just when
we thought we had her hooked
really well.

Jesus Christ, my God, is
coming back to earth. That's a
fact. The moment He comes will
be a surprise to us all. To many, it
will be a shock that He showed up
at all. To the unsaved, Jesus' second
coming will be an eternally fatal shock.
To those who claim Jesus, He wants to find us
loving, forgiving, helping, and telling others about
Him. I think if we only knew the time, that is
exactly what we would be doing. It could be today.

tip

Always wet
your knot
before cinching it
down tight.

AUGUST 27

ROMANS 10:11

As the Scripture says, "Anyone who trusts in him will never be disappointed."

OUR FISHING EQUIPMENT has become so reliable. I have Shimano reels that are several years old and have thousands of hours fishing on them. They still cast and work great, and I trust them in any tournament.

What about people? How many folks do we know who never disappoint us? Not many, if any, but I have a God I can trust in every situation, all the time. He has never let me down before and never will in the future. I need Him the most when the people I trust let me down. We will fail and disappoint each other; that is the sin in us. When that happens, run to God as quickly as you can. He is always ready with answers to your hurts.

tip

Buy a more powerful trolling motor than you think you will need.

AUGUST 28

ROMANS 14:19

So let us do what makes peace and helps one another.

AS THE NIGHTS BEGIN to cool, most bass will start
to move into shallow water. It is amazing how
shallow these bass will roam. I am talking
inches of water—not feet. Their primary
target is small bluegill and perch. They
sometimes literally run the baitfish
out onto the bank. Because some
of the summer schooling is still
intact, these bass roam in bunches
and actually help each other trap
the bluegill against the shoreline.

†ip
Muddy springtime
rivers turn into great
fish catching color water
in late summer.

Our daily goal should be to
constantly help each other.
We should help each other for the sake
of godliness and not for what we can gain.
Just try to imagine what kind of families we could
have, what kind of businesses, what kind of
churches, if we would all just follow this one bit of
godly instruction.

AUGUST 29

MARK 11:25

"When you are praying, if you are angry with someone, forgive him so that your Father in heaven will also forgive your sins."

SOME OF THE BEST trout–fishing holes in this country are really difficult to reach. I have friends who will hike five or six miles to get to these remote honey holes. I know one person who is hiking fifty miles roundtrip this weekend to catch golden trout, and the top altitude is 13,000 feet. Now that is a difficult fishing trip!

An even harder thing to do is pray for someone who has really made you mad or done you wrong, but God says this kind of prayer is a requirement, not an option. Often, the person you are praying for continues to do you wrong. My wife prayed for a man one morning this week, and later that day he sued us. Remember, though, your prayer is as much for your benefit as it for the person you are praying for.

+ip

Try rigging the same crankbait with different line sizes to fish different depths.

2 CHRONICLES 20:15

"The battle is not your battle, it is God's."

ONE OF THE BEST WAYS to get a youngster hooked on fishing is to hook the fish, hand the child the rod, and let them battle the fish. Most kids will learn quickly they are not actually catching the fish, but the important thing is that they are having fun.

We all have battles as we go through life. My preacher, Dr. Andy Bowman, says either you've just fought a battle, you are in one now, or one is just about to happen. That pretty much pegs the slip sinker.

We can fight, or we can let God fight. That choice is ours, but it takes a pretty mature Christian to hand the battle to God. Save yourself some trouble and give your next battle to God right away.

tip

On a really good piece of structure, try several different casting angles.

MATTHEW 14:30

When Peter saw the wind and the waves,
he became afraid and began to sink.

THE TRICK TO CASTING accurately is to
concentrate on the structure you are trying to
throw near, around, or through. Don't fix your
eyes on the spot where you want your lure
to land; look at what's near
that spot.

We all know that Peter
began to fail when he looked at
the wind and waves (the
problem) and took his eyes off
Jesus (the problem–solver).
What a great lesson: success
with Jesus, failure without Him.
That really sums up God's entire
plan about mankind. What do you
want to accomplish today? Fix your eyes
on Jesus. You and I might never walk on water or
accomplish the impossible, but then again, with
Jesus, we just might!

†ip

If you don't use
a fly rod, try fly fishing
with a long light
spinning rod.

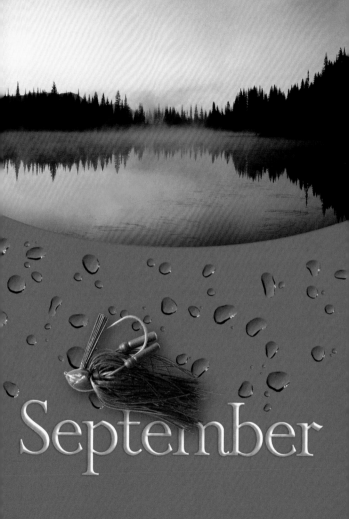

September

LUKE 9:41
*Jesus answered, "You people have no faith
and your lives are all wrong."*

GOOD SPAWNING ACTIVITY every year is essential
for our lakes to maintain good fish populations in
today's heavily fished waters. Spring rains create
the problem. When lakes rise, beds already made
are too deep to receive adequate sunlight. Beds
built at the highest water levels are
killed out when the lake level
drops back. Wrong spawning
conditions can be devastating.

Does a wrong level of faith
affect the way we live? YES,
because it places our confidence
and trust in something other than
the God we must have faith in.

Like water that's too high or too low,
this invariably will lead our lives in the
wrong directions.

If your life is not heading the way you want it
to, check out where your faith is.

† i ρ

Try a Zara Spook
over deep water in
the fall.
Bass will move
several feet to
get the bait.

1 CORINTHIANS 7:23

You all were bought at a great price, so do not become slaves of people.

MY FRIEND GREG BROOM probably has cooked more fish than anyone else I know. He sells a fish batter mix and cooks samples at every Bass Pro Shop opening or event. I guess he has fried literally tons of fish. We recently were talking about *The Passion of The Christ* DVD selling 4.1 million copies in one day—amazing. Greg said even more amazing was that anyone would go through all that pain and suffering for Greg Broom and for Jimmy Houston. But Jesus did, and realizing that should make us want to please Him in all aspects of our lives. The things of this world, the sins of this world, the people of this world, have no ownership on born–again Christians. Let's live like it; the price has been paid in full!

† i p

The more erratic
you work your bait,
the better.

SEPTEMBER 3

DANIEL 9:18

We do not ask these things because we are good,
instead, we ask because of your mercy.

MY SON AND I dove hunt every year the first week
in September. We have been doing this as long as I
can remember. I guess Jamie started going with me
when he was seven or eight years old. The amazing
thing is we kill a limit every single day we hunt
every year. Why? Because we are really good shots?
No—because we hunt where there are lots of birds.

Can we claim blessings and benefits from God
because of how good we are? No, our God has lots
of mercy. God's goodness, not yours or not mine,
is what life is all about. Thankfully, God's goodness
and mercy is plenty sufficient. It is
all we need in all circumstances.
And you can count on that mercy to
last throughout eternity.

tip

Watch your
locator for a
thermocline during the
hotter months.

PSALM 31:7

I will be glad and rejoice in your love, because you saw
my suffering; you knew my troubles.

MY GRANDDAUGHTER, JORDYN, is a fish–kissing
little rascal. She has been kissing fish
since way before she was big enough to
actually catch fish. Her favorite—bass,
of course. We were cleaning a few
small bass this week to eat, and
she had to kiss every one before
I filleted it even though that last
kiss might be just a little late to
show her love.

†ip

Try a gold and
black Cordell Hot Spot
in flats where
shad are present.

God has kissed us with His
blessings. He's always standing by to
help because He loves us! His love is not
based on whether we deserve it or not. In fact,
most of the time we don't. He always knows what
we are going through and will never let us suffer
more than we can bear. Rejoice today, heavenly
help is on the way.

SEPTEMBER 5

ISAIAH 42:21
The LORD made his teachings wonderful,
because he is good.

WE STUDY BASS FISHING because we want to be more successful at catching bass. We watch television shows, read books and magazines, and attend seminars, all to achieve greater success. We assume the teachers are sharing their best information with us.

The Bible is the most helpful instruction book ever written. Called the Book of Life, it certainly is that. Life present, life past, life future, and life eternal.

Everything God wrote in His Bible is for our good. From our work habits to our eating habits to every relationship we will ever have, God has laid down teachings for our benefit in all situations. We only need to claim them.

†ip
Study land contour
as you drive down
the highway.
Imagine it covered
with water.

LUKE 8:50

*"Don't be afraid. Just believe,
and your daughter will be well."*

MY PREACHER, ANDY BOWMAN, told of an 86–year–old deacon he served with in Florida. This man was saved at age sixty. His wife died when he was seventy, and shortly thereafter, the deacon himself was diagnosed with terminal cancer and given only a few months to live. He told God he was ready to go. But God told this old deacon He still had things for him to do and would cure the cancer. He went back to the doctors and told them he wasn't taking any treatments, because God had said He would cure him. They ran more tests, and sure enough, the cancer was gone.

Just like when Jesus walked this earth, God is in the healing business. He asks only that we just believe and not be afraid.

Tip
Bass will move to the tips of points to feed.

DEUTERONOMY 31:19

I am offering you life or death, blessings or curses.
Now choose life!

IF YOU GAVE A BIG OLD FAT BASS the choice of
hitting a hot skillet or being kissed and released,
which do you think she would choose? I am going
to bet she'd rather avoid the hot grease no matter
how bad a kisser you are. Yet God has given us just
that same choice, and many do indeed choose the
frying pan. Why is that? Is it too difficult or too
simple to believe? It is simple! Do you feel
you are not worthy? Well, you're not!
Does it cost too much? Jesus has
already paid the price—in
advance! Do you not have the
time for God? Eternity is
forever! That fish we hold in
our hands is at our mercy for
life or death. We are at God's
mercy, but unlike that bass, the
choice is ours.

tip

Only kiss bass
of the opposite sex.
I never kiss
boy bass!

HABAKKUK 2:4

Those who are right with God will live by trusting in him.

THERE ARE MANY WAYS to fish a Road Runner. All can catch fish. There are really a lot of combinations of Road Runners. I suppose hundreds, when you consider size, color and type of tail. Any can be right depending on the situation. Each can also be equally as wrong.

There really is no wrong situation for depending on God to get things right. No illness, no money problem, no hurt relationship, not even death. We are simply to live by trusting Him. Easier said than done? You bet it is, but the only way any of us can be part of God's power is by going through some times so tough, we can't handle them alone.

†ip
Never overlook
a shady bank,
no matter how small the
shaded area is.

SEPTEMBER 9

REVELATION 3:20

"Here I am! I stand at the door and knock."

THIS TIME OF THE YEAR, bass start chasing quite a bit. The fall feed is beginning and bass are fattening up for the winter. When that old bass chases, he is telling us exactly where he is and usually what type lure to catch him on.

For the Christian, Jesus is always telling us how to please Him. No matter where we are or what we are involved in, He will always make sure we hear Him. We can't be in a storm too loud or in a crowd too rowdy for God not to be heard. We can, of course, ignore Him, and much of the time we do, especially if we are doing something we shouldn't.

Rest assured, though, Jesus will speak to us, and we will be a whole lot better off if we will just listen and obey.

tip

Use deep-diving crankbaits on underwater ledges in late summer and early fall.

EXODUS 23:20

"I am sending an angel ahead of you, who will protect you as you travel."

IF YOU WANT TO CATCH BASS on deep structure, find the underwater routes they travel—roadbeds, creek channels, ledges, and edges. Locate their stopping spots, bridges, brush piles, foundations, and the like. Be on that stopping spot when the fish are, and bingo, you're a hero!

We're a traveling society. I have about two million miles on Delta alone, plus a bunch on other carriers. Probably more prayers are offered up for and by travelers than anyone else. I pray for safety on every flight as well as every trip by land or sea. Do these prayers work? Of course! I don't know how many angels God has dispatched for my family and me, but it must be a lot. Need an angel today? Ask God— He has plenty.

tip

Bass will position below undercut banks up river during the summer and fall.

September 11

ECCLESIASTES 5:18

They should eat and drink and enjoy their work,
because the life God has given them on earth is short.

TIM MCGRAW SINGS a country song about
finding out you have a terminal illness. One of the
things the lyrics tell you to do is take more time to
go fishing. The moral of the song is to live like you
are dying. As I grow older, it makes more and
more sense to me to make every day special.

On September 11, 2001, nearly three
thousand lives ended unexpectedly.
I often wonder what each person did
the weekend before. How many
were saved and are in heaven?
How many were lost and will
spend eternity in hell? God tells
us to enjoy life, enjoy our work,
enjoy each other. He knows we
will have problems, so God warns
that life is short and to make the most
of it. Get out there and make today special
for you and for those around you.

tip
Always experiment
with lure speeds.

COLOSSIANS 4:2

Continue praying, keeping alert,
and always thanking God.

I HAVE TRAVELED BY AIR every year since 9/11 on
September 11th until this year. This year, I flew
on September 12. I really did not give it too much
thought except in 2002 when our pilot came on
the speakers and asked us to buckle our safety belts
and have a moment of silence for the anniversary
of the attack.

Terrorism is probably here to stay, but
Jesus still is the answer. As we pray to Him,
we must thank God for keeping us safe while
we're on the watch for unusual and suspicious
behavior around us. Those of us who fly
a lot may have a greater responsibility,
but we must always pray, stay alert,
and thank God.

tip

Single blade
spinnerbaits are easier
to fish at
deeper depths.

SEPTEMBER 13

2 CHRONICLES 20:20

"Have faith in the LORD your God and
you will stand strong."

BUZZBAITS PRODUCE big fish in the fall. You will
miss several strikes and bites may be few and far
between, but if you will stick with a buzzbait,
especially if you have a little wind or rain, you
have a great chance of catching a
really big bass.

Faith in God is what living a
Christian life is all about. Like
that buzzbait, we will have

✝ip

There are
always fish
in shallow water.

problems and at times God's
blessings will seem few and far
between. But we are guaranteed
to catch the big one—Heaven!
This faith in Jesus does give us the
strength to stand firm when
everything and everybody around us
seems to be crumbling. Faith is our foundation to
lean against when we start to topple. If you ask
God for anything today, make it a request for
more faith.

MATTHEW 4:17

"Change your hearts and lives, because the kingdom of heaven is near."

THE HURRICANE SEASON plays havoc with the fishing in Florida and all along the East Coast. It also makes a mess of things in Louisiana and Texas at times. The damages far outweigh the benefits, but some changes in land and water can help fishing later on.

As Christians, we know that whatever storms hit us in life, there's a big benefit coming later—Heaven! If we positively knew Jesus was coming back tomorrow or next week or next month, how would we feel and act? What would you and I do differently? How would we rearrange our schedules, our priorities? The truth is, Jesus just might come back tomorrow, and He warns that our hearts and our lives need changing. Where can we start? The first place might just need to be with our relationship with Jesus Himself.

tip

Use a shad-colored crankbait if the current is flowing.

LUKE 9:13

"We have only five loaves of bread and two fish, unless we go buy food for all these people."

WHEN YOU LOOK at some of today's fishing heroes on television, you see tremendous fishermen with celebrity status and great influence. Early on, though, they were considerably something other than superstars. Bill Dance was a furniture salesman, Roland Martin was a fishing guide, and my friend Hank Parker was somewhat of a hippie. (God did clean him up pretty good, though.) God has the power to make a lot out of a little.

If Jesus can feed five thousand men with a couple of tilapia and five biscuits, what can He accomplish with you and me? Whatever circumstances you are in, whatever your dreams and goals are, never ever leave Jesus out for a single moment. He has the ability to turn you into a tremendous person.

†ip

In deep water, if your line stops falling, set the hook.

ROMANS 9:24

We are those people whom God called.

MANY OF THE TOURNAMENT GUYS call local tournament fishermen to learn about lakes with which they're not familiar. Most locals are really excited when a big name pro calls them for help.

If you are looking for something to really get excited about, think about who called you to be a Christian. Who chose you to be one of His? No one less than the God who created the world. If you get to feeling your life is falling apart, no one loves you, no one cares, remember whose family you belong to. Would you get excited if Roland Martin, Larry Nixon, or Woo Daves called? This is infinitely better. Start jumping for joy—God Himself has called.

† i ρ
A slider head jig
will give a worm
more action than
a slip sinker.

September 17

PSALM 11:5

The LORD tests those who do right.

IN ORDER TO FISH professional bass tournaments, all you need to do is pay an entry fee. In order to fish at the highest level of BASS or FLW, you must qualify. You are tested at the lower levels before you can play with the big boys.

We don't have to pass any test to become a Christian, but once we join up, we are tested often. We are tested in order to be molded into the kind of Christians God wants us to be. God doesn't need mamby–pamby Christians. He wants and uses Christians who have been tested by whatever life can throw at us. We're forged into Christians with patience, perseverance, humility, forgiveness, generosity, and gratefulness. Mature Christians are tough and know how powerful our God really is.

†ip
If you fish
from the bank
use a Smartcast wireless
Fish Finder.

PROVERBS 28:10

Those who lead good people to do wrong will be ruined by their own evil, but the innocent will be rewarded with good things.

PONDS REACT THE SAME in the fall as in the spring. Fishing improves more quickly in ponds in the spring, because the water warms up earlier than in larger lakes. Reverse that in the fall—that's right, water in ponds will cool more quickly. This sets off an early fall feeding frenzy.

†ip
Pay close attention to the small details in fishing.

The Bible tells us not to hang around with non–Christians, and the smaller our faith is, the more quickly it will be warmed or cooled by the good or bad people we're around. God knows that one bad apple can ruin the barrel and that one evil person can certainly lead many Christians astray. We need to be on the lookout for the devil masquerading as a friend determined to lead us into trouble. Keep in mind, we have a reward waiting.

SEPTEMBER 19

LUKE 12:58

"If your enemy is taking you to court,
try hard to settle it on the way."

IT IS PRETTY COMMON knowledge that I intended
to be a lawyer. One of my college degrees is in
political science. I have said many times that God
saved me from being a lawyer. Praise God, He made
me into a fisherman and let me make a living at a
really super–fun job. Jesus knew long ago how
messed up the legal system would become.

He knew the greed of man would turn
the justice system into a money–bent
paper chase. He knew about
frivolous lawsuits and the desire
of mankind to blame others.
But He also gave us some great
advice that doesn't cost us
five hundred dollars per hour.
Do we need to get rid of all the
lawyers as Shakespeare suggested?
Probably. Must we follow the advice
of Jesus? Absolutely!

tip

Sweep your rod
when casting
a Carolina rig.

JAMES 1:2

When you have many kinds of troubles, you should be full of joy, because you know that these troubles test your faith and this will give you patience.

RUBBER FROGS HAVE BEEN USED for years around heavy grass and lily pads. The Snag–proof frog has been the most popular, but now Zoom and others make some great imitation frogs. The trend also has changed as to where to fish these baits. We now fish them just about everywhere—around docks, brush, rocks, stumps, logs, you name it! One thing remains the same, though: to be successful fishing a frog, you must be patient.

Does God really want us to have real joy everywhere—in troubles, around hurtful people, off by ourselves? Yes, He does! God is a creator and He is continually at work in us creating someone better. It may not be easy to be full of joy during difficult times, but I can attest that it is worth it.

tip

Experiment with new techniques when you are not under pressure to catch fish.

MATTHEW 5:6

"Those who want to do right more than anything else are happy, because God will fully satisfy them."

IT MIGHT BE IMPOSSIBLE to satisfy a largemouth bass. They can eat so much that they keep on feeding even when their bellies are bulging. Thank goodness they don't have to be hungry to strike a lure.

Being satisfied is something we all want. We desire to be satisfied with our families, marriages, jobs, friends, our churches, but complete satisfaction comes only from God. All else will leave us empty and wanting more. God's rule is that our desire must be to do what is right, and He will satisfy us because of that desire. Does this mean He will give us everything we think we need? I don't think so! It does mean that we will be satisfied with whatever we have.

tip

A high-speed reel
will allow you
to slam a crankbait
into underwater cover.

PROVERBS 28:25

A greedy person causes trouble, but the one who trusts in the LORD will succeed.

ONE OF THE BEST PLACES to find a school of bass this time of year is on a ledge, creek channel, or point. Bass school on these spots to feed when shad get active. If you can get one bass to bite, the others often will get greedy and go into a feeding frenzy. Great for you, trouble for the bass.

Greed is difficult for most of us. There's a fuzzy line between greed and ambition. We all want success, and often success and greed are measured by what we have. I believe greed is actually measured by what it costs you, not by what you have. Greed is what you are willing to pay (or give up) to get what you want. God says that success comes from trusting Him. Oh, how simple!

Tip
Shad will get active on man–made lakes when current begins to flow.

SEPTEMBER 23

HAGGAI 1:13

Haggai, the LORD's messenger gave the LORD's message to the people, saying, "The LORD says 'I am with you'."

MY CAMERA MAN PAT TURNER, who runs our production company, gets lost on just about every lake we fish. If I ever die out there, and I just might on a really great strike, Pat probably won't find his way back to the ramp. He faces backward when we are running the boat, and he is looking through the camera lens while we are fishing. He doesn't worry about where we are, because he is sure I can always find my way back.

When we belong to Jesus, we never need to worry about being lost or being alone. In the deepest, darkest night or in our most desolate or trying situation, the Lord promises, "I am with you." It doesn't take long after you are saved to realize just how important and comforting God's presence really is.

† i p

Use a fire–tiger
Hot Spot where
muddy water mixes
with clear water.

ISAIAH 43:4

Because you are precious to me,
because I give you honor and love you.

IF YOU ARE A BEGINNING FISHERMAN or if you
are teaching someone to fish, don't dwell on what
you are doing wrong. At the same time, be sure to
learn from your mistakes. If there is a fisherman
out there who doesn't make mistakes, I've never
been in the boat with him or her.

God knows that we make mistakes in
our relationships with Him and with
others. He knows we sin even after we are
saved. We know, however, that He loves us
and that we are more than just important to
Him—we are precious to Him. We all
want to be loved. We want to be
special to someone. How humbling
and yet incredible it is to know
that we are very special and loved
so very much by the God of the
universe. He said so Himself.

†ip

When willow bushes
get flooded, break out
your spinnerbaits,
no matter what
time of year.

LUKE 7:50

Jesus said to the woman, "Because you believed, you are saved from your sins. Go in peace."

WHEN THE BITE GETS really tough, what is the best tool you have? Whether you go to light–line and small finesse baits or your heaviest flippin' stick in the densest cover available, your best tool is . . . CONCENTRATION. You must really believe you will get a bite on the next cast.

Believing that Jesus is the Son of God, that He died on the cross for your sins, and rose again to life and is living in Heaven now is the most important belief you will ever have. Concentrate on Him. You have a choice, and no one can make it for you—not your mom or dad, your spouse, or your preacher. This is between you and Jesus. Peace here on earth and peace forever in Heaven. Jesus paid the price and is holding out that nail–scarred hand; just take hold and believe.

†ip

Visualize how your lure is working under the water.

1 CORINTHIANS 4:13

When they tell evil lies about us, we speak nice words about them.

THE CHANGING OF A SEASON is always exciting for fishermen. The fall is particularly exciting because it leaves behind those dog days of summer. As we watch the water temperature drop we see our success ratio go up. The fall also brings the political season or, as some people call it, the lying season. I am shocked at how easily most people lie. It's like people think God has removed telling lies from His top ten list of sins. Today's verse really caught me by surprise, and I have had the chance to put it into practice several times recently. As you might suspect, the benefit has been to me. I cannot tell if my saying nice words has had any effect on the ones doing the lying, but it has given me some peace. Try it yourself and let me know.

† i p
Don't be afraid
to cast deep and
bring your bait shallow.

PHILIPPIANS 4:12

*I know how to live when I am poor, and I know
how to live when I have plenty. I have learned the secret
of being happy at any time in everything that happens.*

MOST OF THE NEW BREED of bass tournament
fishermen operate under the belief that things will
change every day. To be successful, you must learn
to adapt with the changes. Start with a plan, but
realize that the solution to each day's success is a
moving target.

The Apostle Paul had the solution to happiness
in everything—rich or poor, free or imprisoned,
hungry or full, beaten or praised. He had learned
the secret. That secret for Paul was Jesus. That secret
is there for us, too. Paul got his
strength from Jesus and knew that
with Christ his joy was not in
physical being or circumstance.
His joy was Jesus Himself. All else
really pales in comparison,
whether it is the most wonderful
thing we can imagine or life's
most dire circumstance.

†ιρ

Reeds close
to the deeper water
will produce
bigger bass.

JOHN 16:24

*"Ask and you will receive, so that
your joy will be the fullest possible joy."*

WHY DO WE SPEND so much time helping others
learn how to catch fish? Why are we so patient and
understanding with our wives and kids in that
teaching process? Why do we take a friend fishing
who really doesn't know how to fish? We do these
things so that those we love can experience the
same joy in fishing that we do. That is exactly
why Jesus is so willing to give to us. He is
willing to give whatever it takes so we
can experience the joy He has in
Heaven. It is a joy that we cannot
even comprehend—the fullest
possible joy. He is also concerned
about the daily joy we have in
our short time here on earth. He
filled His Bible with His word to
make sure we can find that joy,
no matter what.

✝ i ρ
Stop or pause
a frog in any "hole"
or "opening"
in lily pads.

MATTHEW 5:12

*"Rejoice and be glad, because you have
a great reward waiting for you in heaven."*

HAPPINESS IS A TEN-POUNDER! Yes, indeed. In
fact, for me, it doesn't need to be nearly that large
to put a big smile on my face (and a pucker on my
lips). I have heard so many fish stories and most
end with . . . *I finally caught that really big fish,
a fish of a lifetime.*

What God has waiting for us should
keep our bobber of happiness and joy
floating high at all times. Jesus says it
is a great reward, and He should
know. He came from Heaven
and is there right now waiting
for us to show up. He told us
this in advance so we would
have something to really look
forward to when times get
tough. When your bobber starts to
sink a little, set the hook and think
about that reward that Jesus has waiting.

✝ i p

Troll points
with a Hot Spot
or deep-diving crankbait
to locate fish.

PSALM 34:19

People who do what is right may have many problems, but the LORD solves them all.

WHEN I THINK BACK to the early days of tournament fishing for Chris and me, it seemed like life was a constant struggle—raising two babies, starting a career, paying bills, and playing in this new deal called bass tournaments. All the while, we were trying to develop a strong relationship with each other and with the God we both trusted so much. I never thought I would say it, but indeed, those were the "good old days." Now our struggles include several businesses with more than a hundred people working who need a regular paycheck. We deal with bankers, lawyers, customers, suppliers, sponsors, friends, and even a few enemies. Most people are really a blessing. The God who Chris and I trusted as teenage newlyweds is still right there solving our problems, one by one, and that trust is even greater now.

tip

Bass normally suspend in cover and not on the bottom.

October

OCTOBER 1

LUKE 19:10

*"The Son of Man came to
find lost people and save them."*

HOW DO YOU FIND a bass that weighs only a few
pounds in a body of water that covers
thousands of acres? You learn to go where
that bass lives. Where did Jesus look to
find sinners needing to be saved?
He went where they lived. Praise
God, He came looking for me.
It is surprising to think Jesus
would leave Heaven for any
reason. It is even more astounding
that He came here to be rejected,
humiliated, beaten, and crucified just
to pay the price for the sins He knew I
would commit. Would you leave your home
to pay for a murder someone else committed?
Would you suffer beatings for lies you didn't tell?
How about letting nails be driven into your hands
for adultery you had no part of? Well that is what
Jesus did and a billion times more.

† i ρ
The older and
trashier a boat dock is,
the better it is
for fishing.

OCTOBER 2

ISAIAH 33:6

He will be your safety. He is full of salvation,
wisdom, and knowledge.
Respect for the LORD is the greatest treasure.

CHRIS AND I HAVE BEEN CAUGHT in many storms, many times, on many lakes. When I think back, we have outlived several cats with nine lives. Yes, we have had some close calls and sure, we were scared, but our God has always been our safety. God is so awesome, and He deserves and commands our respect in every way possible. This respect is not for God's benefit, it is for ours. Only when we store up this respect can we partake in His salvation, His wisdom, and His knowledge. True wisdom and knowledge come only from God.

Try adding a request for wisdom and knowledge to every prayer. Give God a chance to let these grow in you. As they do, your treasure chest of respect for God will become even fuller.

†ip

Picture in your mind how a bass is positioned on a piece of cover.

PROVERBS 22:4

Respecting the LORD and not being proud will bring you wealth, honor, and life.

WE PARTICIPATE IN MANY EVENTS for kids, and it is always a thrill to see a youngster catch a fish, especially if it is their first fish. They beam all over, and their mom and dad are so proud of them. So when does that accomplishment turn into pride, and why is pride bad? God says pride is bad and can rob us of so much He wants us to have. I believe pride comes when we think we are better than someone else. That is not God's way. Our example is Jesus. He served and honored others. He serves and honors you and me every day. We need to think of others as more important than ourselves. Wouldn't it be wonderful if we Christians would think of each other this way!

tip

Big bass are lazy. Use big, slow-moving lures to catch these hawgs.

OCTOBER 4

ISAIAH 40:28
The LORD is the God who lives forever,
who created all the world.

WHEN BASS ARE HOLDING TIGHT to cover, we want to fish great target baits like jigs, worms, and spinnerbaits. During the fall, with cooler water, bass start to roam. Very similar to what I use in February and March, a Cordell Hot Spot becomes my favorite bait. I still throw at the bank, make a lot of casts, and cover a lot of water. The fish will be scattered and not holding around structure.

God created a changing world, yet God never changes. There is precious little that we can count on in this life, but we can always count on God in all seasons, all situations. The God who created us will never die, and He has promised that we will live forever with Him. I'll take that deal!

† i ρ
Learn to half–step
a Zara Spook.

2 CORINTHIANS 5:21

Christ had no sin, but God made him become sin,
so that in Christ we could become right with God.

RON LINDER, AL'S BROTHER, is one of the nicest
guys I know. He is also a strong Christian and
shares his faith on a regular basis. Ron and Al are
so different. Ron is a tough (but gentle) guy who
you would want on your side if a fight broke out.
Al is the polished, ever–smiling, fast–talking TV
fisherman who we all love. Together, they
became some of the most successful
fishermen ever. God has used their
differences and different personalities for
their benefit. He also has made them the
same to Him through their faith and
belief in Jesus. God sees us all as saved
sinners because of Jesus.
Nothing else, and I mean nothing
else, really matters.

✝ip

Replace any
negative fishing thoughts
with positive thoughts.

OCTOBER 6

GALATIANS 5:22

The Spirit produces the fruit of love, joy, peace, patience, kindness, goodness, faithfulness, gentleness, self control.

WE GET TO TAKE A LOT of people fishing. Kids, older people, celebrities, politicians, singers, CEOs, preachers—people from all walks of life—and my primary goal with each is to make sure they have fun. My job is a piece of cake because of what God's Holy Spirit has given me. Looking individually at each "fruit of the Spirit" I see how each plays a major role in fishing with someone, often someone I have met for the very first time.

Study these "fruits" and see how important they are in your relationships with your spouse, your children, your boss, your employees your enemies, and even people you meet for the first time today. Jesus promises eternity, but He gives you the tools to live great day by day.

tip
Transition fishing line
(that changes color)
will help you
catch more fish.

EPHESIANS 6:12

Our fight is not against people on earth
but against the rulers and authorities and spiritual
powers of evil in the heavenly world.

FISHING IS SOMETIMES more about fighting
the natural elements rather than figuring
out the fish. This is especially true in
tournament fishing where we must
compete no matter what the
conditions. Often if we can
overcome the bad weather,
changing water conditions, or other
circumstances, we can succeed.

†ip
Crappie begin
to move shallow again
at this time of year.

Many of the struggles and
problems we face in life create great
battles. But what are we really fighting?
Bad personal relationships, money problems,
co–workers, companies, lawsuits? According to
God, our adversary is none of the above. It is the
devil himself and his legion of demon angels.
Do we have the strength, power, or ability to fight
this battle ourselves? I think not, but I know One
who does and His name is Jesus!

ECCLESIASTES 7:29

"God made people good, but they have found all kinds of ways to be bad."

DURING THIS TIME OF THE YEAR, a lot of our lakes have what we call "glop" on them. This glop forms a solid surface in shallow water and around docks, laydowns, and stumps. I like to fish a spoon on top of this glop. The spoon leaves a trail so you can actually see what you have fished. Bass miss the spoon often and leave a hole in the glop. Have a worm or jig handy to throw in that hole, and it is generally a sure fish every time.

Like that bass strike messes up the top of the glop, we all find ways to mess up God's good creation—us! We sin, no matter how hard we try or how holy and righteous we think we are. We are so fortunate to serve a God who sent Jesus to pay for our mess.

tip

The strike zone of a bass enlarges as a weather front approaches—use faster-moving lures.

PROVERBS 16:24

Pleasant words are like a honeycomb,
making people happy and healthy.

ONE OF THE KEY THINGS to remember about a
brush pile is that the brush usually spreads farther
around down there than you think. After you have
fished a brush pile—not before—spend several
minutes perusing the pile with your fish locator.
See if you have any brush sticking out the side or
maybe another good piece of brush close to the
main pile.

Pleasant, kind, and happy-sounding
words also go a lot farther than you
can ever imagine. What would your
words be if Jesus Himself walked
into the room? I know my
countenance would brighten in a
heartbeat no matter how bad my
day was or how big my problems
seemed to be. Well, He is in the
room right now.

tip

Learn to read
and interpret
topographical maps.

OCTOBER 10

JOSHUA 1:9

"Don't be afraid, because the LORD your God will be with you everywhere you go."

DURING A TOURNAMENT PRACTICE on Lake Russell in Georgia, Chris and I had caught several good bass up to seven pounds on a couple of bridge crossings. We caught these fish buzzin' a spinnerbait just a few inches below the surface. During the tournament this didn't work at all. I started slowing down my bait until I was literally crawling that spinnerbait along the bottom. Bang! The fish finally bit the bait. I caught a great limit every day. I didn't need to run all over the lake. The fish were there all along, and I just needed to adjust to them. Jesus is always right there with us, no matter what changes around us. We must not fear. God will provide and He is anxious to do so. We just might need to adjust our attitude a bit.

†ip

Fish both the outside and inside edges of weed beds.

MATTHEW 13:50

"The angels will throw the evil people
into the blazing furnace, where people will cry
and grind their teeth in pain."

HOMER CIRCLE, the legendary outdoor writer,
penned a prayer that ends with him asking to
be judged big enough to keep. Ron
Linder talks about being scooped up
by the gentle net of God's grace.
Every Christian should
unquestionably understand that
God practices "catch and keep"—
not "catch and release."
Irrespective of what God is doing
in your life or mine, the key reason
to be saved is to keep from being
thrown into hell. Heaven and hell are not
states of mind, they are very real places. Heaven is
as good as it could ever be, and hell is as bad as it
gets. We each have an appointed time to die and
leave this earth. We will spend eternity somewhere.
I choose Heaven; I choose Jesus.

tip
My favorite jig
color is a
black/blue/purple
combination.

OCTOBER 12

PHILIPPIANS 4:19

*My God will use His wonderful riches in Christ Jesus
to give you everything you need.*

ROCKS AND ROCK PILES can be great places to fish,
especially if you have a lake that has few rocks.

Lakes with rocks and rocky banks and ledges
everywhere can be tough. In fact, on such lakes
I concentrate on non–rocky cover like docks or
wood. Those occasional rocky spots can really be
hot spots. By the way, a Cordell Hot Spot
is a super bait to fish on rocks.

There will always be rocky times
in everyone's life. God knows this,
and we might as well accept it.
The key is that God knows
exactly what we need to get
through these times, and He has
promised to supply what we
need, even if it's not all that
we want. Look back at some of
your rockiest times and remember
how God gave you exactly what you
needed to make it across those rocks.

†ip

Have a worm
handy to "follow up"
missed strikes on
topwater baits.

MATTHEW 16:18

"On this rock I will build my church, and the power of death will not be able to defeat it."

SMALLMOUTH FISHING IN the Great Lakes and upper Northeast can get really easy if you can locate isolated rocks. A decent-size rock will hold a smallmouth or two under just about any conditions. Good polarized sunglasses are a must. Try to fish the shady or undercut side of the rock if possible.

tip

Engage your reel on a buzzbait the instant the lure hits the water.

When Jesus told Peter He would build His church on a rock, He wasn't calling Peter that rock, even though the name "Peter" means "rock." The rock Jesus would build on was His death, burial, and resurrection to conquer sin. The church is not made up of buildings, but of people believing in the Gospel. Without that rock of Jesus' resurrection from death, there would not be a church. Is Jesus building in you, or are you just warming a pew?

JOHN 8:11

*"I also don't judge you guilty. You may go now,
but don't sin anymore."*

AROUND THE TOURNAMENT weigh–in sites we have
off–limits areas where we are not allowed to fish.
There are probably more daily disqualifications for
this rule violation than all other rules combined.
It is pretty cut and dried; you are either
guilty or you're not! It is usually an
honest mistake, or at the very worst,
a dumb mistake. No one fishes the
off–limit release areas intentionally
to cheat. They are just mixed up
as to where the boundaries are.

Sin is sin, whether committed
on purpose or unintentionally.
All sin must be paid for or
punished. That punishment is eternal
damnation in hell. Praise God, He sent
Jesus to pay the price so we can avoid the
punishment for going outside God's boundaries.
Jesus says, "I don't judge you guilty." For this, we
certainly should "sin no more."

†ip

Bass in clear water
rely more on sight
and can see lures more
than thirty feet away.

ISAIAH 13:11

The LORD says, "I will punish the world for its evil and wicked people for their sins.

FALL FISHING IS FANTASTIC pretty much all over the country. As the water cools down, shad move into creeks, and bass and crappie get really active on points. It is also a time of great changes in weather—severe weather like tornadoes and hurricanes, fires, floods, and drought. The 2004 hurricane season was the worst ever for America. Is God trying to tell us something? Is what's happening all around us a warning that this country needs to come back to God? If so, it doesn't appear we are paying too much attention to Him. Most people didn't listen to what God was telling them through Isaiah either, but everything God warned about happened. God is true to His word. America must change to continue to exist.

† i p

A bone-colored crankbait with an orange belly works well in muddy water.

JEREMIAH 15:11

The LORD said, "I have saved you for a good reason."

CLEAR WATER IS PRETTY much defined as being able to see a white lure down four feet deep or more. The combination of clear water and cooling temperatures is great to fish large-bladed spinnerbaits. I like a half-ounce Terminator with a #5 to #7 round Oklahoma blade. Best skirt colors are bubblegum and perch color. Bulge the water with the big blade and get ready for some killer strikes. This combination works because bass have adapted to the clear water.

We are saved by God because He has a clear purpose for our lives. I believe God has a purpose for each of us *every day*. How disappointed He must be when we fail to recognize the opportunities He gives us. What purpose does God have for you today?

tip

Slow down and concentrate on where you want your lure to land and how you want it to work.

HEBREWS 12:4

*You are struggling against sin, but your struggles
have not yet caused you to be killed.*

MUDDY WATER IS A STRUGGLE for many
fishermen, especially those who are not used to it.
Anglers who fish primarily clear lakes are often
stymied when water looks like Yoohoo. Here in
Oklahoma and those states around us, we thrive
on muddy water. Bass are more object–oriented.
Slow down with jigs and spinnerbaits and put
those lures in the heaviest cover you can find, and
muddy water will get a whole lot easier.

Most of us struggle to be the
Christians we want to be. We fight
against the mud of anger, harsh words,
envy, jealousy, greed, slander . . .
and this list merely scratches the
surface of our list of personal sin.
This struggle is daily, and it is
difficult, but it is a battle God
wants us to fight. I think He sees
us as better Christians down
the road.

tip

In the fall,
the most important
thing to a bass
is food.

PSALM 128:1

Happy are those who respect the LORD and obey Him.

I HAVE MANY "RULES OF THUMB" in fishing.
There are rules I follow wherever we are fishing.
One simple rule is: bigger baits catch bigger bass.
Another rule is to fish a spinnerbait at a depth
just before it goes out of sight. You need to have
your very own set of "rules" to fish by. They can
be quite a bit different than mine, but they must
have a foundation of facts and experience.
Follow those rules and you'll catch more fish.
　　Although the Bible is not a book of rules,
He has given us commands and instructions
in it that we must follow to be happy.
My "rules of thumb" help me catch
more fish. God's "rules of thumb" are
designed to give us a fuller, richer,
more complete life.

†ip

Use a 36-volt
trolling motor if you
want to cover
a lot of water.

JOB 36:22

"God is great and powerful; no other teacher is like him."

I USE A STRONG 24–volt MinnKota Trolling motor on my Tracker boats and a super–powerful 36–volt on my Rangers. I use the strongest trolling motors that MinnKota makes, over one hundred pounds of thrust. I always want the most powerful with the very best batteries so I can fish under any conditions and can stay on that trolling motor all day. I demand the very best, even though I need all that power only during a small part of my fishing day.

I also serve a mighty, powerful God. He is a God so great that no matter how difficult the conditions become, He can plow right through them. I might not need all of God's power every day, but it is always available and just waiting to be turned loose.

†ip

Search out areas
that have both deep
and shallow
water potential.

MATTHEW 15:11

*"It is not what people put into their mouths that
makes them unclean. It is what comes out of their
mouths that makes them unclean."*

HAVE YOU EVER FOUND shad, bluegill, or crawfish
in your livewells? Not a pretty sight! Those are
baitfish that bass have spit up. You can see how
different they are from what they were just a short
while earlier. They have gone from being
something beautiful to something really ugly.

We spit up a lot of bad stuff in our lives, too.
Things like gossip, backbiting, lying, and malice.
God knows that the bad things that come out our
mouth can really cause us trouble. When we get
mad or jealous or envious, we are
apt to say things we don't really
mean and for which we will later be
ashamed. The most gracious
people I know always seem to
pause before they speak. Maybe
they are thinking about what
they say before they say it
instead of after it is already said.

†ip

Small bodies
of water can produce
really big fish.

PROVERBS 21:21

Whoever tries to live right and be loyal
finds life, success, and honor.

WHEN WE STARTED WITH ESPN about twenty
years ago, my main concern was simply staying on
the network. ESPN was not really that big back
then, and I just didn't know much about the
people. They were from the North, I'm from the
South, so I just hoped we could get along. Our
relationship has been great and longstanding.
I believe the key is that ESPN is very loyal to
their show producers, and I also have
been very loyal to them. We have
worked together to do things
correctly, and it has been good for
us both.

    God sees loyalty as extremely
important. It starts with loyalty to
Him and being loyal to our
spouse, our kids, our church, our
employer, our friends. It might seem
better to "cut and run" sometimes, but it is
not God's way.

†ip

Bass tend
to scatter when
water levels rise.

OCTOBER 22

MATTHEW 25:13

"So always be ready, because you don't know the day or the hour the Son of Man will come."

I BELIEVE MY FIRST merit badge as a Boy Scout was for fishing. In fact, I qualified for that badge several times over. What really digs my memory from scouting was the Scout motto—"Be Prepared." Just think about how many fewer mistakes we would make if we daily followed that motto. We would certainly have less credit card debt, be healthier, and have more money set aside for retirement or those rainy days. Jesus Christ is coming back. Are we ready? Is our relationship with Him strong enough today if He appears tomorrow? The world was not ready for Jesus when He first came some two thousand years ago. I don't think it's ready now, either. As Christians, we must be ready, and we can—one Christian at a time.

✝ip

Hot lead weights heated by the sun can damage your fishing line.

JAMES 3:13

Are there those among you who are truly wise and understanding? Show it by living right and doing good things with a gentleness that comes from wisdom.

AS BASS GET BIGGER AND OLDER, they do indeed get wiser and more difficult to catch. One of their tricks is to feed mainly at night. Another is to spend most of their time about ten feet deep, a depth that a lot of fishermen don't fish.

> tip
>
> Swim a jig around boats in floating docks, even in deep water.

In life, we are supposed to get more wisdom and understanding. What we do with these gifts is up to us. God says we show these gifts by the way we live. We do good for those around us, and we must indeed "mellow" with age. I am a hard–charging guy, but I do want wisdom. I want understanding. If God grants these requests, I must realize that along with wisdom and understanding come some pretty big responsibilities, especially in living right.

OCTOBER 24

ISAIAH 12:2

*God is the one who saves me; I will trust him
and not be afraid.*

AS HOOK MANUFACTURERS have developed
sharper and sharper hooks, I have begun to use
smaller hooks. In my worm fishing, I have moved
down more than one hook size. I am now
routinely using 1/0 and 2/0
hooks where we once used
4/0 hooks. I have learned to trust
those smaller, sharper hooks.
I learned that trust by trying
them out and catching lots of
bass on small hooks. Obviously,
the smaller hooks give the
worms better action and produce
more strikes.

We learn to trust God by trying
Him out as we live through situations that
demand His help. It is difficult for most of us to
really trust God until we have seen Him in action.
Like catching a lot of bass, I have seen God work in
my life a lot of times.

†ip

Learn how deep
your lure will run
with different line size.

ACTS 17:31

God has set a day that he will judge all the world with fairness, by the man he chose long ago.

TO FOLKS NOT DIALED into tournament fishing, some of their first questions always involve fairness. They know fishermen lie. How do we keep these guys and gals from cheating? Harold Sharp, the wise tournament director for BASS, always said the judge is in the other end of the boat. Tournament anglers are actually policed by the competitors in their boat. We are, in fact, required to report any rules violations.

†ip

Choose a lure color that matches the background.

God is watching tournaments and everything else we are doing. He sees it all, and Jesus will judge both the world and each of us. On that day, only saints will ask for justice; the rest will plead for mercy.

OCTOBER 26

1 TIMOTHY 6:17

Command those who are rich with things of this world not to be proud.

FISHING IS A GAME that doesn't care who or what you are. To the fish, a person of privilege in a $40,000 Ranger boat is pretty much the same as a barefoot ten-year-old fishing off the bank. We will not get to Heaven because of our wealth or poverty. God freely gives His grace to all. However, He does expect more out of those of us to whom He has given more. He expects us to use the things of this world for the benefit of others. This includes tithing and much more. It includes using your talents, your property, your vehicles, your money, whatever God has given you. Our biggest trap is trusting in what God has given us rather than trusting in God. This trap will always lead us into great danger.

tip

Shad will move to the very tail end of creeks in the fall.

JOHN 20:29

Jesus told him "You believe because you see me.
Those who believe without seeing me will be truly happy."

ONE OF THE MOST NATURAL PIECES of cover
that fishermen sometimes pass by is a tree that has
fallen in the lake on a really steep bank. The tops
of such trees may be lying in water as deep as
fifteen or twenty feet or more. This actually
provides both deep and shallow cover for the fish,
plus everything in between. I slow roll a
Terminator spinnerbait or drop swim a jig all the
way from the bank to the treetop. Often this
takes a really long cast. We cannot see the
top ends of the trees, but we know they
are there. It's obvious.

Many people who looked Jesus
in the eye and heard Him speak
didn't believe Him. They missed
the obvious. What a mystery
that is, and how glorious it will
be when you and I come face to
face with the one who saved us.

†ip

An outgoing tide
usually produces
clearer and better
fishing water.

OCTOBER 28

MATTHEW 26:64

"In the future you will see the Son of Man sitting at the right hand of God."

I WON'T ARGUE ABOUT whether fall fishing is better than spring fishing, but it is pretty hard to beat a dead calm October morning with that touch of coolness in the air. That's my Rebel Pop R time. With steam coming off the water, let that bait lie still until every ripple disappears. Don't twitch that rod tip much; just a small plop–plop is all you need. A little spit from the nose of that bait and BANG—game on. If that is not pretty close to Heaven, I'll eat your Pop R! One day, many of us will stroll into Heaven and we will see Jesus, that one who died for us. Tragically, some people will not be there. God has invited everyone. If you have not accepted Jesus as your Savior, don't wait another day.

✝ip

Try fast–moving
lures in clear water

PROVERBS 24:12

He is watching you, and He will know.
He will reward each person for what he has done.

MOST OF A FISH'S LIFE is centered around only two things: eating and not being eaten. For a short period of time each year, they are concerned about spawning or raising babies, but then it is back to focusing on food and not becoming food. Everything else is secondary.

Because we know God is always watching, all–knowing, what should our lives be centered on? For some of us, our focus is the same as the fish—food—but our lives should revolve around God and what He wants for us. Godly living, godly loving, godly caring, godly sharing, godly attitudes. The Bible says God has a reward for each of us, and I am pretty sure it is not shad for dinner.

†ip

Fish a spinnerbait at a depth just before you lose sight of it.

OCTOBER 30

1 PETER 4:14

When people insult you because you follow Christ, you are blessed.

THE BEER PATCH SITUATION has been widely publicized in both Christian and non–Christian circles. Most stories center around the points I lost, the money passed up, the chastisement received, or how I was hurt or penalized by not wearing that patch or placing the beer decal on my boat. What has been missed is all the blessings my God has showered down because of it. The publicity has given me even more opportunities to share Jesus' Gospel than ever before. We have been in more churches and talked to more non–Christian sportsmen than ever before. There are men in Heaven right now who made that important decision to accept Jesus during one of these events. When we suffer, God has all the ability in the world to turn that into great victory.

✝ip

Always try
to make your
first cast to a
target perfect.

ROMANS 8:14

*The true children of God are those who
let God's Spirit lead them.*

MOST OF US LEARNED to fish from Mom and
Dad. Fishing is a family sport, and most parents
who fish get a lot of pleasure teaching their
children about it. We also have a tendency to
like the same lures and types of techniques that
our parents like. If Dad likes buzzbaits, we like
buzzbaits. Dad has instilled that in us.

That is what God wants from you and me.
He wants us to act and react just like He would to
everyday happenings in our lives. How would God
react if He was fired, sued, cheated, lied to,
divorced, left out, or badmouthed?
By praying in the Spirit that God has
placed in all of us who are saved.

†ip

Bass are lazy;
make it easy for them
to "eat" your lure.

November

PHILIPPIANS 2:14

Do everything without complaining or arguing.

MY GRANDCHILDREN—Jeremy, Kyle and Jordyn—
have all been exposed to great fishing experiences.
They have fished out of the very best boats made.
They have had the very best rods and reels in their
hands with the best lures tied on the ends of
the very best lines. Of course, they get to
fish in water teeming with fish, yet they
start complaining pretty quickly if
they don't get a bite. The youngest
one, Jordyn, is the worst.
She complains even more if
someone else is catching fish and
she isn't. Childish? Sure, but don't
we carry this childish behavior
into our adult lives? You bet we do.
And that is not at all what God
wants. When you catch yourself starting
to complain about something today, talk about
a blessing or two instead.

†ip

Pick your bait
for the spot and
type of cover
you are fishing.

NOVEMBER 2

ISAIAH 49:16

"See, I have written your name on my hand."

AT OUR KEYS HIGH SCHOOL football game this week, my granddaughter, Jordyn, got into one of her "Granddad's autograph" modes. She was having me sign programs, paper cups, and anything else she could find. Of course, she had all of her little friends doing the same. When they ran out of things, they proudly presented their hands. I obliged by signing with a permanent marker and now have several moms mad at me, including my daughter–in–law.

Think about having your name written on the hand that formed you, the hand that created the oceans. You can't get any more special than that. Just think, God looks down and sees your name right there every day.

†ip

Larger line works
better on a
Pop R or a Zara Spook.

HEBREWS 13:20

*I pray that the God of peace will give you every good
thing you need so you can do what he wants.*

WHEN YOU HEAR PROS TALK about making a milk
run in tournaments, what do they mean? A milk
run is laying out a tournament day where you
systematically stop and fish several different spots.
Each spot must have something that you believe
will allow you to catch at least one fish there.

My God has promised to give us exactly what
we need to excel in this milk run of life so we can
do His will. Whatever talents, whatever skills,
whatever money or time we have are direct gifts
from God. He also has given us the
choice to use all these gifts for our
glory or for His. How can you use
your good things today to do what
God wants?

tip

You can pretty
much stick to a jig in
cold muddy water.

PROVERBS 3:30

Don't accuse someone who has not harmed you.

ON A REALLY LARGE LAKE, one of the easiest
ways to locate bass is to find a major creek that has
everything a bass needs. That creek becomes the
entire lake for the fish because they never leave, no
matter the conditions or the time of year. They feel
safe, have places to spawn, and have plenty of food.

A sin that has everything it needs to dwell in
our spirits and haunt us is when we say something
bad about others. Most of the time,
we've spouted off about a situation
that has not hurt us and often one
where we are not involved in at
all. I have been on the
receiving end of accusations
coming from folks I didn't
even know and who were not
involved. The hurt and pain
are very real. Let us hold our
tongues (and our e-mails) and
remember that this is a sin that creates
unnecessary pain to others.

tip

Small holes
in matted cover
should be fished with a
pegged slip sinker.

JAMES 5:13

Anyone who is having troubles should pray.

CASTING ANGLES CAN BE just as important as
locating fish. Most of the time, we are around
some fish, but catching them can be tricky.
I think it is really important for a
fisherman to stand up when bass
fishing. This will dramatically
improve your angles to your target,
especially if you are flippin',
pitchin', or making short casts.

†íρ
Bass actually hear
(feel vibrations)
with their lateral line.

It is really important for a
Christian to pray in order to
flourish in life. God knows what
we are going through. He knows all
the angles on every situation. We are
not praying to let God know what troubles we
have; rather, we are praying to include God in the
problem–solving. God wants to be the solution,
not just a part of it. A great deal of the time,
I find I have a problem because I left God out in
the first place.

PHILIPPIANS 2:5

In your lives, you must think and act like Christ Jesus.

DID YOU EVER WISH you could think like Roland Martin, Larry Nixon, Bill Dance, Kevin VanDam, or Hank Parker? What if you had the fishing knowledge of all these men stored inside your head? Then all you would need to catch fish would be the water.

How about thinking and acting like Jesus Himself? That opportunity is available, and it is far better than having the know–how of all the superstar fishermen put together. Jesus experienced everything you and I will ever face. He struggled against the same adversary, the devil, and He conquered. He died, just as we will, and His resurrection proved we can and will live again also. He has given us His very Spirit so we too can be like Jesus.

t i p

Choose a crankbait that will run deep enough to hit some structure or cover.

1 JOHN 4:4

God's Spirit, who is in you, is greater than the devil,
who is in the world.

OCCASIONALLY SOMEONE GETS into my boat
who is particularly foul–mouthed. This is a little
rare, but when it happens, their words really stand
out. Usually that person will apologize but will
continue to slip from time to time throughout the
day. It is a pretty safe bet that God's
Spirit does not live in that body.
But even if God's Spirit is present,
I believe the devil is constantly
trying to push God out and
claim a little territory for
himself. I know I let the devil
win some ground at times. The
problem is that if we let the devil
get his foot in the door, he will try
to kick the door down and take over
our whole house. Thankfully, we have a
weapon. That weapon is God's Spirit, and if we use
it, it will send Satan running every time.

tip
Standing up
while fishing will allow you
to see more
underwater cover.

2 THESSALONIANS 2:13

Brothers and sisters, whom the Lord loves,
God chose you from the beginning to be saved.

IT IS FUN TO WATCH the non–boaters at our pre–tournament pairings. Most have paid their entry money in hopes of drawing Denny Brauer, Roland Martin, or another of the big name superstars. You can see people's elation when they do and also their disappointment when they get someone they have never heard of. We should be overjoyed to learn that God has chosen us to go fishing with Him. We should also be very thankful. So thankful that we work extra hard to be obedient to Him. In order to please God, we must work extra hard to love each other and forgive one another. No matter how tough life gets, no matter how big our problems, just think— God chose us. That is not only bigger, it is better than anything this world has to offer.

tip

If it is important
to the fish,
make it important
to you.

1 PETER 5:4

Then when Christ, the Chief Shepherd, comes, you will get a glorious crown that will never lose its beauty.

WHEN I FIRST SAW a Terminator spinnerbait, it was and still is, the prettiest spinnerbait I have ever seen. The gold-plated blade was shinier than any other on the market. The fish-like metalized head was awesome and looked so real. The quick-change skirt with two sizes of rubber tails had incredible action. It was really more a work of art than a fishing lure. The frame was made of Space Age titanium. I was, to say the least, very impressed.

As pretty as that Terminator looked, it will not come close to what God has in store for you and me. Not a halo, but a crown more glorious and more beautiful than we can ever imagine. And, unlike the spinnerbait that gets pretty ragged after forty or fifty bass, our crown will look just as amazing after a thousand years.

†ip

You can tell if the tide is going in or out by looking at weeds or anchored boats.

JAMES 3:16

Where jealousy and selfishness are, there will be confusion and every kind of evil.

ONE OF THE WAYS TO FISH a large flat is to drift and simply drag your lure behind the boat. This works well with a Carolina Rig or a tube. On lakes like Sam Rayburn in Texas, we have flats with irregular bottoms. Drifting works great in these areas. I always keep a marker buoy handy and pitch it overboard when I get a strike.

Although we are saved, most of us have a tendency to drag sins along with us for a long time. One sin that is hard to leave behind is jealousy. It is hard, many times, to feel good about someone else's success, particularly if it is someone you compete with. God says jealousy produces evil. He equates jealousy with evil. Most of us don't look at ourselves as evil, but what does God see?

+ i p

Most bass in rivers can be caught less than four or five feet deep.

NOVEMBER 11

GALATIANS 3:28

*In Christ there is no difference between Jew
and Greek, slave and free person, male and female.
You are all the same in Christ Jesus.*

AT A SPORTSMAN'S JAMBOREE recently in
Columbia, South Carolina, I had the chance to
tour the historic First Baptist Church where the
event was held. The gorgeous new sanctuary holds
over three thousand people. What intrigued me,
though, was the original sanctuary where the
pastor, Wendell Estep, explained the seating.
The lower area was for the free men; the upper
seating, a surrounding balcony, was for the slaves.
The platform where the preaching was done was at
a height an equal distance between the
two seating areas. This signified that
even though men separated
themselves, God sees no
difference. Praise God, His
impartiality is exactly what
allows you and me to be saved.

†ip

Make your casts
upstream when fishing
in current.

NOVEMBER 12

1 CORINTHIANS 13:7

Love patiently accepts all things. It always trusts,
always hopes, and always remains strong.

FISHING IS A PARTICIPATION SPORT. Over sixty
million Americans fish. Some of these sixty million
like to fish, but most LOVE to fish. Those of us
who love fishing patiently endure whatever the
sport throws at us. Bad weather, bad lakes, bad
partners, and even the dreaded "lockjaw" when the
fish refuse to bite. We still love, we still hope.

God has commanded us to love each other
no matter what. He did not recommend we love or
suggest we love—He *commanded* it. With this
godly love comes huge commitment to each other,
and this commitment includes
forgiveness. If you harbor anything in
your mind that requires forgiveness,
do it right now. For love to remain
strong it must accept all things,
including wrong, and forgive.

tip

Use desiccant packets
in your tackle box
to help eliminate
moisture and prevent
rusty hooks.

*"If you do things well, I will accept you,
but if you do not do them well, sin is ready to attack you.
Sin wants you, but you must rule over it."*

THE ELEMENTS PLAY A BIG part of any day's
fishing. Most of the perfect days occur when we
have to work and can't go fishing. Wind, rain, hot,
cold, high water, low water, muddy, clear . . . every
situation can pose a problem. The better fisherman
you become, the more you will be able to use
different circumstances for your benefit.

God expects us to excel. He wants us
to succeed and do things well in every
circumstance. He will not abandon
us when we don't do as well as we
should, but He does give a
warning. When we goof off,
sin will be there to pounce on us.
We either rule over sin with God's
help, or sin will rule over us. Is there
something you can do today for God's
benefit or for others? Go out and do it.

†ip

Wind direction
will predictably position
bass on structure
or cover.

Catch of the Day | 335

November 14

HEBREWS 13:5

Keep your lives free from the love of money and be satisfied with what you have.

CLEAR WATER IS A LOT OF FUN to fish, but it can be pretty frustrating if we are not willing to change our tactics a bit. The simplest way is to move to light line, four– to eight–pound test, and small lures. My choices are one–eighth–ounce spinnerbaits, tiny crankbaits, Blakemore Road Runners, and four–inch finesse worms. These small lures will produce fish and lots of strikes, but you will need to be satisfied with smaller bass.

Most of us have a hard time being satisfied with less. It's hard not to want or pursue money. We work harder and longer hours. We change jobs. How do we balance our needs, our family's needs, and still please and obey God? We must be satisfied with what God gives each of us, because the most important part of life is not money, it's Jesus.

†ip

Use a shad–colored spinnerbait when fall water temps drop to the low to middle 60s.

HEBREWS 12:25

So be careful and do not refuse to listen when God speaks.

I HAVE ALWAYS BELIEVED we would one day have underwater speakers, perhaps attached to our trolling motor, that would transmit sounds under the water to help trigger strikes. Maybe we could talk with the fish using the sound of active shad or schooling bass. I am actually using such a unit right now called Biosonix, and I have had some pretty positive results.

Is God talking to His people today? Yes! Does He talk to us individually? Yes, again. During my most trying and difficult situations, my God has always been there. He talks to me as I pray, listen to sermons, read His word, or worship Him with music. He has given me answers, reasons, and comfort. I could not make it without Him. Trust me, God will speak—just listen.

tip

Catch shad below dams for great catfish bait.

NOVEMBER 16

1 PETER 3:13

If you are trying hard to do good,
no one can really hurt you.

IF YOU SPEND MUCH TIME with fishermen, pro or
amateur, you will soon hear stories of bad days
turning into huge victories. You find this true in
just about any profession. Most everyone fails a lot
before they succeed. Keep on trying hard and never
give up. In fishing tournaments, they never keep
score of all the casts that didn't get a strike. They
only put on the scales the ones that did.
Jesus wants us working hard at doing
good, no matter what results we are
getting. He even says we cannot
really be harmed as long as we
are working hard to benefit
others. We wonder why bad
things happen to us when we
are working so hard to do God's
work. Don't get frustrated; don't
give up. Jesus has your victory just
around the corner.

tip

Your first cast
in a brush pile
should be
on the edge.

ROMANS 11:5

There are a few people that God has chosen by his grace.

IN NOVEMBER 2004, America chose its president. They chose one of my fishing friends, George W. Bush. Long before America re–elected George W. Bush; long before his dad was president; even long before I first met George W. in Pine Bluff, Arkansas, when his father was the vice president, God chose George W. Bush. He chose him for something much greater being than president of the United States. God chose him to be saved from hell to be with Him in Heaven.

　　Chosen by God's grace. We need only to accept that grace, so freely given. Our president has accepted that grace. I have accepted it. Have you?

†ip

Willowleaf blades allow your spinnerbait to get deeper quicker.

MARK 4:24

"The way you give to others is the way God will to you, but God will give you even more."

WE SPEND SO MUCH TIME with our grandchildren. Fishing, hunting, birthday parties, ballgames, and just being with them. We often revolve our entire schedule around them. No matter how much time, how much attention, how much love we give, we seem to always get back more. God says it will be that way with Him. We cannot out–give God. Many believing Christians have tested this, and I have yet to hear it not come true. Help others, and see how much God helps you. Increase your tithes and offerings, and see what God does. God is a rewarding God. He has our greatest reward ready and waiting—Heaven! He also has plenty of rewards to give us right here on earth.

†ip

You can turn a floating jerkbait in a suspending jerkbait by simply adding Storm Suspendstrips.

NOVEMBER 19

DEUTERONOMY 4:34

He did it with tests, signs, miracles, war and great sights,
by his great power and strength.

THERE ARE MAYBE MILLIONS of unfished bass in
the United States. We have more small pieces of
water available that have never had a bass lure
tossed into them than you can shake your
favorite spinnerbait rod at. Most of the
water holes are around cities and towns.
They are around shopping centers,
golf courses, housing developments,
abandoned gravel pits, and other
unsuspecting spots.

We might overlook some
super fishing holes, but we
cannot possibly overlook the
awesome power of an almighty
God. God displays His great power
everyday. Even a non–believing
outdoorsman sees this. To those of us who are
believers, we not only see these miracles and great
sights every day, we have come to rely on them.

† i ρ

Add a split–shot
to small spinnerbaits
for easier casting.

November 20

TITUS 2:8

Speak the truth so that you cannot be criticized.

WHEN THE WATER TEMPERATURE starts really dropping in the winter, the temperature you want to really watch for is 58 degrees. When the water hits that magic number, bass will generally be most active. This is probably the best spinnerbait temperature you will see until springtime. Once the water temperature falls a few degrees blow 58, bass fishing will become more difficult.

Complete truthfulness is a "magic" quality to develop in your personal and professional life. In today's world, this a rarity. personally know only a few people I can count on to tell me the truth under all circumstances. When you are tempted to bend the truth a little or just flat outright lie—don't.

†ip

Try to not let your shadow fall onto a target you are fishing.

LEVITICUS 18:26

"You must obey my laws and rules and you must not do any of those hateful sins."

LIKE POINTS ARE TO A LAKE, wing dams are to a river. If you know nothing else about a lake, you can go from point to point and have a good chance to catch fish. Do the same with wing dams. They always hold bait, have rock and wood cover, and direct the way the current flows. The breaks and cut–out areas almost always will produce eddies where fish will wait for something to eat.

God's laws should direct the currents of our lives. As long as we live according to how He tells us to live, we will have few problems. Break these rules and we must suffer the consequences. God doesn't want to see us hurt or suffer. He wants to see us happy. The happiest you and I will ever be is when we are faithfully obeying God.

†ip

For extra color, try a red Daichi bleeding hook as your trailer hook on spinnerbaits.

NOVEMBER 22

JAMES 5:16

When a believing person prays, great things happen.

AS BASS BECOME LESS ACTIVE when the water cools into the fifties or lower, we need to both slow down and make our lures a little more compact. I like the new tungsten Terminators this time of the year. I can get the bait deeper more quickly, and the small frame bait will get a few extra strikes, especially in clear water.

When difficulties arise in our lives and the lives of people we know, prayer is the key. God is always in the active mode of answering prayer. Every believer can testify to answered prayer. I have friends alive today because of answered prayer. Never, and I mean never, underestimate what God has the power to do. Never stop praying.

†ip

Nose hook
a finesse worm
on a drop shot rig
on smooth bottoms in
ultra–clear water.

1 PETER 2:9

You were chosen to tell the wonderful acts of God,
who called you out of darkness into his wonderful light.

BASS FEED AT NIGHT and are easier to catch.
Really dark nights, though, are all but impossible
without some help. Lights of some kind—from
boat docks, black lights, or even the moon finally
peeking over the mountains—are both welcome
and extremely necessary. Without God, it's like
our very being is groping around on a pitch black
lake. Jesus is the light that brightens our lives.
He lights us up so we can lead others to Him.

If you are saved, God is doing some great
things in your life right now. Share that with
someone today and watch God
brighten up their world.

tip

Learn the
"fishing-line" trick
for easy hook removal
from just about any part
of the human body.

GENESIS 15:6

Abram believed the LORD, and the LORD accepted
Abram's faith, and that faith made him right with God.

THIS WEEK I FISHED with an eleven–year–old
named Austin in Alabama. He knew so much
about fishing and hunting that it was like fishing
with a small adult. He learned most of this
knowledge from his granddad.

I love to fish with kids
because they hang on every little
bit of instruction and believe
what you are teaching them is
absolutely true.

We are all little children to
God, and what He has to teach
us is one hundred percent true.
All God asks is that we believe.
We believe with all we have and
know that God is able to accomplish
everything He has promised. It is this faith that
makes us right with God. What a great Granddad
we have in this God we serve.

†ip

Learn to
make short,
accurate casts.

MATTHEW 5:16

*"You should be a light for other people.
Live so that they will see the good things you do
and will praise your Father in heaven."*

TOURNAMENT FISHERMEN LIVE for recognition.
Magazine articles, television, radio, newspapers,
Internet, anything to get their names out there.
Some have big egos, but most just need the
recognition to promote their current sponsors and
attract new ones.

As Christians, we should be walking,
talking billboards for Jesus. Everything
we do and say should shine a bright
positive light on our Savior, Jesus
Christ. Oftentimes, my light
shines pretty dim. When we
think of what Jesus did for us,
how He helps us every day, and
what He has prepared for us, how
can we justify anything less? Let's
make today a day that showers praise
on Jesus by the way we live it.

† i ρ

Fish depend
more on smell and
sound in
muddy water.

NOVEMBER 26

PSALM 42:1

As a deer thirsts for streams of water,
so I thirst for you, God.

THE BIGGEST DEER I have ever taken with a bow
in Oklahoma came when I was just a teenager.
It was a twelve–point with massive horns and long
tines. I shot the buck about forty–five minutes
before dark. I had been in the tree since before
daylight. The key to success that day? It was an
extremely dry year and I was hunting a small pond,
the only water in the entire area. Every deer for
miles around had to come to that water.

Jesus called Himself the Living Water. He is,
in fact, the only Living Water available for you
and me. For eternal life, we must come to Jesus.
He is our only option.

†ip
Try shortening
your plastic worms
under tough conditions,
even down to
three or four inches.

PROVERBS 10:12

Hatred stirs up trouble, but love forgives all wrong.

MY WIFE, CHRIS, is a great fishing partner and a
great partner in life, and whatever challenges
come against us, we face them together.
Not everyone is so blessed. Hatred probably
develops during a divorce more than at
any other time, but love is indeed
blind. God made love so strong,
so powerful, that it absolutely has
the power to forgive the most
grievous of wrongs we do to each
other. This is a gift from God,
and it is exactly how God loves us.
His love is so great, so binding,
so eternal, that no matter how bad we
are, He forgives. He has provided Jesus to make
our marriage to Him complete. He's the partner we
all can always count on.

†ip

A GPS unit on the
bow of your boat
will give you
an extra advantage.

1 CORINTHIANS 13:13

So these three things continue forever: faith, hope and love. And the greatest of these is love.

WHEN YOU HAVE BEEN FISHING and living with the same woman for over forty years, you learn a great deal about love and just how powerful God really made it. As I look back and realize just how much I love Chris today, I wonder if I was really in love at all forty years ago. I am sure I was, but love is like a rubber plant that grows beyond our wildest imagination. I could never imagine loving a woman this much, and I miss her almost immediately when we are apart. As great and strong as that love is, I believe God's love for her and for me is even greater. God's love was carried all the way to the cross some two thousand years ago, and I believe it has grown every day since.

tip

A snap attached to the split ring will give a jerkbait a wider wobble.

1 CORINTHIANS 3:9

We are God's workers, working together;
you are like God's farm, God's house.

I HAVE ALMOST AS MUCH FUN managing my
fishing lake as I do actually catching fish.
I spend a lot of time making the fishing better and
the fish bigger and more productive. We fertilize;
we feed; we build spawning areas; we haul shad; we
add cover; we do whatever it takes to improve all
aspects of our lake. Shouldn't we get just as excited
about working for the God who has done so much
for us? Together we can feed, love, teach, forgive,
lift up, encourage, and improve everyone around
us. We can and should make a difference
for God every single day of
our lives. The most amazing
thing is that when we make a
difference for God, He will make
an even bigger difference for us.

✝ip

Fish into the sun
whenever possible
to avoid
casting a shadow.

1 PETER 1:7

These troubles come to prove that your faith is pure.

BASS FISHING, ESPECIALLY tournament fishing, is definitely a moving target. In order to really stay at the top of the game, you must fish every situation as it comes to you. We must actually fish the day, the hour, the moment, and even each cast according to a wide range of variables. To figure out these variables, we rely on our skills, abilities, and experiences. Troubles, like changes in fishing, come along regularly. They come as a check on our faith. Is our faith strong enough to rely on God, or do we run from God? I have learned that I must rely on God. The bigger the problem, the more I need God. After all these years my God has never failed me . . . not even once.

tip

You can add glitter to a blade or crankbait with clear fingernail polish.

December

DECEMBER 1

JOHN 11:44

The dead man came out, his hands and feet wrapped with pieces of cloth, and a cloth around his face.

MOST PEOPLE WHO FISH from boats have long since given up carrying fish stringers. Some younger bass anglers probably don't even know what a stringer is. We now use sophisticated livewells and chemicals to keep our fish alive. Today's verse is about the famous Lazarus. Dead for four days and smelling bad, Jesus raised Lazarus with just three words, "Lazarus, come out!" This is the business Jesus is all about—renewing life—but before He raises us from physical death, we must admit this death and ask forgiveness to receive this spiritual life. Jesus is a life–giver, and if you haven't yet received that life, you need to do it today.

tip

You can change the depth of a crankbait by simply raising or lowering your rod tip.

JOB 33:12

"God is greater than we are."

IT IS PRETTY EASY to listen and pay attention if Jay Yelas or Roland Martin starts talking about how to catch bass. Most people believe these pros know more about catching bass than they themselves do. Listening to their buddies in their bass clubs is a different story. What causes this? Pride, unbelief, the feeling you know more than the other guy does? But what if he really can help you?

How often do we do think we know more than God in our daily struggles? The last time I checked, God is still God and I'm not. He is also more powerful than the most awesome thing or event we could ever imagine. Do we really think we could do a better job without Him? Try God today. Include Him in every aspect of your life today, and then survey the results tonight.

tip

Don't be afraid to try new lures, techniques, or ideas.

DECEMBER 3

HEBREWS 12:1

So let us run the race before us and never give up.

YOU WILL NEVER HEAR a champion fisherman say he knew he was beaten after the first few hours of competition. Always believing and never stopping are the keys to success in whatever we are doing. Life is certain to throw many roadblocks in front of us. Troubles will come, but God is always able to overcome. We just need to hang in there and do our best with whatever God has equipped us. God will always reward our efforts. Will we always succeed, always win? In the short haul, victory is a moving target. But in the long haul, for eternity, Jesus has provided for those who believe in Him the certainty of absolute victory. Let's never give up.

†ip

When fishing gets tough, try slipping a piece of Alka-Seltzer inside a tubebait.

PROVERBS 5:21

The LORD sees everything you do,
and he watches where you go.

I KNOW OF VERY FEW fishermen who have not
cast a lure into water where they were not supposed
to fish. Most hunters have ventured onto land—at
least for a few feet—that they were not allowed on.
Would this have happened if the owner or a game
warden was looking on? I don't think so. Why in
the world do we say things, go places, and do
things as if God can't see or hear or know
what we're up to? Surprise! He knows, hears,
and sees everything. We actually should live
our lives in constant awareness of messing up,
and I praise God that in His huge grace
He completely forgives every wrong
that He has ever seen us do.

† i ρ

Larger blades
will give a spinnerbait
more lift.

DECEMBER 5

1 CORINTHIANS 2:5

This was so that your faith would be in God's power and not in human wisdom.

WE SPEND OUR ENTIRE LIVES trying to get smarter about fishing. It is a fact: the more we know about the fish, the water, the weather, and the time of the year, the more likely we will have success. We rely mostly on our own smarts, but often we need help. Trying to solve our problems just by being smart is foolish. The fact is, God generally will let us get deeper and deeper into trouble until we call on Him for help. God requires that we completely trust in Him. He allows us to get into dire situations in order to grow our faith. If all went well every day, we wouldn't need to put our faith in much of anything. Problems grow faith.

tip

The calmer the water, the further a bass will usually travel to get your topwater lure.

1 JOHN 3:18

*We should love people not only with words and talk,
but by our actions and true caring.*

EVERYONE I RUN INTO has a fishing story. Some
are true, but many are not. I have heard most of
the fishing jokes several times. I still listen and I
still enjoy the stories and the funnies. I listen
because I care for the people telling the stories.

We all like to talk—me more than most.
The problem is, most of today's society is not
listening. People are not listening because their
hearts and minds are so centered upon
themselves. They really care about no one else.

If we want to be more like Jesus Christ
today, we simply must listen. This
works at home, at work, at church,
virtually everywhere. It is so
powerful that it will even work
with a total stranger. Listen to
someone today.

tip

In the wintertime,
the afternoon bite is
usually better.

DECEMBER 7

ISAIAH 59:1

Surely the LORD's power is enough to save you.
He can hear you when you ask him for help.

WE TRUST COMPLETELY in God's ability to take us to Heaven, to save us from hell, and give us eternal life with Him. But how much does He care about our problems with our boss, our money, our friends? Is God really concerned when we have a spat with our spouse or get wronged in a business deal? You bet He is! God tells us that if we can be trusted with just a little, He will trust us with a lot. We can certainly trust Him with everything, no matter how big or how small. Whatever our needs, God will always listen. When no one else seems to care, God does. When we are frustrated, God will encourage. No one cares more about us than the God who made us.

†ip

On topwater lures, you can coat the last foot or so of line with fly line dressing.

MATTHEW 19:23

*"It will be hard for a rich person
to enter the kingdom of heaven."*

LUKE CLAUSON WON $500,000 by winning the
2004 FLW Championship. At the tender age of
25, Luke had won in four days more than many
pros had won in a lifetime. Riches, of course, must
be measured in more than money. How can riches
keep us away from God and make it nearly
impossible to get to Heaven? Because wealth so
often rearranges our priorities. God's desire is to be
the only Lord of our life. He will not play second
fiddle to anything, especially money. When we
put God first, He will provide the
riches we need. Even wealth, though,
can be a trap. When God blesses
you with riches, be very careful to
keep these riches in their proper
place—below, not above, God.

† i p

Try a floating
worm on a
weighted hook
in deep clear water.

LUKE 10:18

"I saw Satan fall like lightning from heaven."

RECENTLY, PAT TURNER and I spent three days in Kentucky bow hunting. We experienced some of the most spectacular and severe lightning I have ever seen. Pat was in one tree with a metal camera and a metal camera brace. I was a few feet away in another tree with my metal PSE bow and carbon arrow. We were twenty–four feet high, sitting on a metal lock–on Summit tree stand.

I watched lightning strike in a heartbeat. If God hurled the rebellious devil from Heaven that quickly, how can He stand to look on the rebellion and sin we daily commit? He can't, but He doesn't need to see our sin because of what Jesus has done for you and me. Jesus died to hide our sins from His Father, Almighty God.

†ip

A wacky rigged worm will work even in the wintertime.

HEBREWS 12:2

*Let us look only to Jesus, the One who
began our faith and who makes it perfect.*

I HAVE SAID MANY TIMES that the only perfect
cast is one that comes back with a fish attached
to the end of it. Perfect casts are hard to come
by, and some days they hardly happen
at all.

Jesus is the sole, perfect reason
for our faith. Without Jesus, we
would have no hope of
forgiveness, no hope for grace or
mercy, no chance for eternity,
and no real reason for living.

Jesus is where our eyes must
focus daily to get us through. Jesus is
where we look to handle life's problems, both
big and small. Jesus is a friend when we are lonely,
a safety net when we are scared. Jesus loves,
He heals, He strengthens, He encourages. Is there
really anything or anyone else in whom we could
have this perfect faith?

tip
Build brush piles
in cold weather when
the sap has drained
to the bottom
of the trees.

DECEMBER 11

1 JOHN 1:9

If we confess our sins, He will forgive our sins,
because we can trust God to do what is right.

AT LAKE OKEECHOBEE a few years back, Chris
and I were catching a few bass out of pepper grass
pods on worms. We tried several colors until
Chris hit upon purple with a yellow tail.
This color combination out–produced any other
color by a wide margin. I finished in the top ten
by fishing the right pattern with the right bait in
the right color.

We serve a God who will always
do right by us. He knows the right
pattern for our lives. He loves us
more than we can ever know.
God wants only the best for us,
and when we humble ourselves
and confess our sins, we become
God's children. Even when God
corrects us when we fail Him, we
can most assuredly count on God to
do the right thing for us.

†ip

Bass get very
conditioned to current
and power plant
generation patterns.

2 THESSALONIANS 2:17

God loved us and through his grace, he gave us a good hope and encouragement that continues forever.

ONCE WE LEARN HOW TO CAST, we continually learn how to cast better. The more we learn, the more fish we catch. Fishing is not something we need to re–learn every time we go to the lake.

Once we are saved, we are saved forever and that, of course, goes way beyond this temporal life here on earth. This belief should be our focus every time trouble pops up in our lives. God's grace is our ticket to joy and happiness, no matter how bad things are during our greatest struggles. Instead of dwelling on what is wrong today, we should think about what our lives will be like a thousand years from now. We have a God who loves us immensely, and He proves it every single day. Our job is merely to trust Him and accept that mighty love He so freely gives!

†ip
During cold fronts, bass get into the thickest cover possible.

PSALM 100:3

Know that the LORD is God. He made us, and we belong to him; we are his people, the sheep he tends.

IT IS SO ENJOYABLE to see our kids and grandchildren grow in their fishing abilities. Through time and a great deal of patience we watch them improve, learn, and then become creative in the ways they fish. They go from no knowledge at all to figuring out better ways to catch fish. What a thrill that is to watch.

Our God is constantly watching and looking out for each of us. As we created our kids, He created us. He must really get excited as we grow in Christ. He made us to make Him happy. Our own children are so proud when they accomplish something, and they know we share in their joy. God feels the same way about you and me. Our daily goal should be to make God proud of His creation—us!

tip

Bass will load up under dead leaves in the tail end of pockets in the fall and early winter.

PSALM 147:5

Our LORD is great and very powerful.
There is no limit to what he knows.

FISHING AND HUNTING are built around limits.
Limits are what we use to make these activities
better. Limits for bass have decreased over the years
from ten or fifteen bass down to five or six. Limits
for deer and turkey have, on the other hand,
increased just about everywhere.

Whether we like it or
acknowledge it, God has placed
limits on each of us. He did this
so we can't become God. He is
God, I'm not! God does have
the potential to stretch our limits
far beyond what we can do
alone. And the great thing is that
He wants to!

tip

Just a few degrees
change in water
temperature makes
a big difference
to fish.

When you feel you have reached
your limit in whatever you are trying to
accomplish, ask God to move the boundaries,
stretch them out a bit. I have seen Him do it
many times.

DECEMBER 15

EXODUS 3:12

God said, "I will be with you."

PAY CLOSE ATTENTION TO how deep you hook a fish. This can give you some really good information. If a fish is hooked deep, or swallows your hook, there are probably more fish on that spot. A fish barely hooked might indicate few fish or tell you to make some changes in your lure or your presentation. How a fish is hooked will almost always tell you something. God has told us from Genesis through Revelation that He will always be with us. He has never wavered throughout time. Sure, there have been many times when I have left God, but God has always been there to welcome me back. As I have grown older and hopefully a bit wiser, I try very hard to never leave God out of anything I do. I'm hooked on Him, but even more, He's hooked on me.

✝ip

Fish for snook in salt water with the same lures and tactics you use for bass.

HEBREWS 4:16

Let us, then, feel very sure that we can come
before God's throne where there is grace.

AT THE BASS PRO SHOP Outdoor World in
Toronto, Canada, I visited with many folks who
were planning trips to the South. They were
going to Florida, Mexico, even Oklahoma to go
bass fishing. By contrast, in the South in the
summertime, we get excited about going north
to Canada to fish.

One day, we will go to the most
exciting place there is—the throne of God
Himself. We can approach that throne with
giant smiles, because the throne overflows
with the grace that Jesus has given to His
saved flock. This promise is ours
because of our faith and trust in
Jesus. What a great day and
terrific feeling that will be when
God looks down from that
throne and smiles back.

†ip

Drill holes
in buzzbaits and
spinnerbait blades to
create bubbles.

DECEMBER 17

JAMES 5:9

Do not complain against each other or
you will be judged greatly.

WE HAVE BEEN DOING the Jack Houston Memorial
FOCAS Tournament now for seventeen years. It is
the largest purse tournament in Oklahoma with
over $60,000 in cash and prizes. We use all
volunteer help. One of our main volunteers,
Gerald Halpain, mentioned that no one ever
complains or gripes about anything going on at
this event. The volunteers and the contestants have
the same goals in mind for the tournament—
to raise money for our local FOCAS ministry.
Wouldn't it be great if we did everything
every day in the same manner? Well, we
certainly should, because this is exactly
what God wants and what He has
commanded us to do.

tip

Don't forget to
winterize your
inboard/outboards.

REVELATION 21:8

Those who refuse to believe, who do evil things,
who kill, who sin sexually, who do evil magic,
who worship idols, and who tell lies—all these will
have a place in the lake of burning sulfur.

ONE OF THE BEST PLACES to fish a spinnerbait is
in the heaviest possible cover you can find, the
nastier the better. Get close, make short accurate
casts, and bring that Terminator through that cover
from several different angles. Just a slight change in
angle can often produce strikes.

The worst place I can think of is hell, a literal
lake of fire. Why would anyone refuse to believe
God and therefore have hell as their eternal
destination? Nothing in this life can be
as bad as hell really is. Trusting in Jesus
Christ will totally remove that
destination from anyone's
itinerary. If you're not saved,
don't let another day go by
without making Jesus your Lord.

Tip

Always make
as little noise
as possible in
clear or calm water.

DECEMBER 19

2 TIMOTHY 3:1, 2

In the last days there will be many troubles, because people will love themselves, love money, brag, and be proud.

ARE WE IN THE LAST DAYS, the days just before Jesus comes back to earth? Are things really bad enough? Well, it certainly seems so! Worldwide, magnum troubles do prevail. Individuals, leaders, and countries make their policies and decisions based on money. In America, we are accused of being arrogant and proud. Throughout God's Bible, He prophesies or makes predictions, and all come true. Will we soon see Jesus riding on the clouds, arriving with a shout? Even more important, are you and I ready? I am. If you are not, I would make that my top priority. Today might just very well be THAT DAY.

tip

To stripe a lure, use a comb and spray paint.

PROVERBS 31:28

Her husband also praises her.

I OFTEN BRAG THAT AFTER over forty years of marriage, I am an expert on marriage, perhaps even an expert on women. The truth is, I am only an expert on marriage to one specific woman, and my expertise about her is still in the learning stage. I can tell you guys one thing, though—brag about your woman. Lift her up and praise her every single chance you get. When something bad about her pops into your mind, immediately replace the thought with one of her star qualities, especially if you were about to say something bad to her. And, ladies, live your marriage so that your man has plenty to brag about. Give him lots of ammunition. Raise your star qualities in his eyes to levels he cannot ignore. Marriage isn't tough, it's exciting!

tip
Watch closely
for breaks, baitfish,
and brush
on your locator.

MATTHEW 6:14

"If you forgive others for their sins, your Father in heaven will also forgive you for your sins."

THIS IS THE TIME of the year to break out your "monster" spinnerbaits, those one ounce and heavier. I prefer nickel blades, and my favorite is solid white. Fish these baits deep with non–stretch line such as Fire–Line or Spider Wire. This will give you a great forgiving hook–set, even in deep water.

Forgiveness is contagious. The more you forgive others, the more others will forgive you. It is also pretty easy once you start doing it. If you are harboring any type of malice, ill will, or hatred toward anyone today, simply forgive them. It doesn't really matter how much they have wronged you, forgive them. You will feel better about them and about yourself, and God will feel better about you.

†ip

Florida's best plastic worm colors are red shad and June bug.

DECEMBER 22

LUKE 24:38

*Jesus said, "Why are you troubled?
Why do you doubt what you see?"*

BASS FISHERMEN, particularly tournament anglers, are known for getting help from each other. Even at the highest level we continue to ask each other for help. We simply know that we don't have all the answers in every situation.

After Jesus' resurrection, many doubted and still did not believe what they were seeing. Some found it easier to believe they were seeing a ghost, not looking into the eyes of the risen Savior. But they were seeing Him, and we will also. Jesus is bigger than death, bigger than sickness, bigger than money problems, family problems, and work problems. He is bigger than any situation we will ever face. We need only to believe and not doubt what we see.

tip
Trim and flare
the weed guards
on your jigs
for better hookups.

Catch of the Day
375

ACTS 17:25

This God is the One who gives life, breath,
and everything else to people. He does not need any
help from them; he has everything he needs.

WHY DO SO MANY FISHERMEN give so much time, effort, and money teaching someone else how to be a better fisherman? Why do we give so much to kids, our own and others? Because we care about them? Yes, possibly, but also because giving to others makes us feel better. When we give, we usually gain even more. God has designed our giving to Him as just another way to allow Him to help us. Again, we give, we gain. Whether you are giving your time, your talents, or your money, God will use those to bless you even more. His interest is in your heart; His search is for your motives. When you really give out of the goodness of your heart, I believe you are making God happy.

†ip

Frog pattern lures
work well in small lakes
and ponds.

1 JOHN 3:6

So anyone who lives in Christ does not go on sinning.

ICE FISHING DOES NOT EXCITE me. I have never tried ice fishing, so I cannot really say anything bad about it. But my real fear is that I might actually have a ball doing it. I know a lot of folks in the North who live for the day that the ice gets thick enough to venture out on.

I hate to sin. All Christians should hate to sin, but we all do. So why do we venture into sin after Jesus has saved us? Because we do not live all of our lives in Christ. We are guilty of parceling out our lives to Jesus a little at a time. The parts we hold back keep on sinning. God wants, even demands, that we turn all of ourselves all over to Him. Only then can we really experience all the great riches He has for us.

†ip

To cut down the silhouette on a spinnerbait, remove ten or fifteen strands from the skirts.

DECEMBER 25

REVELATION 22:17

*Let whoever is thirsty come; whoever wishes may have
the water of life as a free gift.*

BIG RAINS PLAY HAVOC with fishing any time of
the year, but they can be particularly troubling in
the winter. If the water is cold and gets muddy, the
bite can get really hard. The solution can be simple.
Go to the upper ends of creeks and rivers until you
find clear water. Here you should be able to catch
bass, crappie, white bass, walleye, or catfish.

My Savior, Jesus, calls Himself Living Water.
He has poured Himself out on the cross as a
sacrifice for you and me. We pay for water that we
drink and use today, but the eternal
life–giving water that is Jesus
doesn't carry a price tag at all.
It is free when you place your faith
in Him.

†ip

Fish feed better
and more often
under a steady
normal barometer.

2 THESSALONIANS 2:10

This will happen on the day when the Lord Jesus comes to receive glory because of his holy people.

THIS IS THE TIME of the year when most tournament fishermen begin to look forward to the coming year. Whether you are fishing weekend tournaments in Oklahoma or Arkansas or fishing the BASS or FLW tour events, you are excited and building on the hope of a great year.

The day Jesus Christ returns to earth is the great hope of all Christians. It is the hope that keeps us going through all the trials, persecutions, and problems we encounter along the way. This hope is real because of what Jesus has already done for us and is continuing to do on a daily basis. Never lose hope; never give up. One of the very best ways to keep your hope alive and strong is to share it with someone who doesn't have it.

tip
Use smaller lures in ponds as most baitfish get eaten before they can mature.

DECEMBER 27

PSALM 130:5

I wait for the LORD to help me, and I trust his word.

I RECENTLY LISTENED to a five–year–old as he told me about going fishing and not even getting a single bite. I asked him how long he fished. With bright eyes and a dead serious look he explained, "I fished five minutes and didn't catch anything." We've all been there. I suppose most of us might be there now with God. We covet God's help, we need God's help, but we want to set the terms. We want to draw up the deal, and we want that help—NOW. God's word has the answer to any problem we need solved. The biggest problem any human can have is being lost without God, without Jesus. I can guarantee that God can solve that problem and He can absolutely do it—NOW.

tip

Downsize your spinnerbaits and crankbaits when fishing current.

PROVERBS 8:8

Everything I say is honest; nothing I say is crooked or false.

THERE IS A SEASON for just about every type of lure. Deep into the colder months, most pros would recommend a jig or a slow-rolled spinnerbait. Good advice, but never be afraid of trying just about any lure in any situation. Remember that I have caught bass buzzing a spinnerbait in a snowstorm in December.

There is absolutely no season whatsoever for lying. Honesty is indeed the best policy. Our entire society in this country is built around lying to each other, and we will forever be under God's condemnation as long as we continue that way. Think you don't lie? Tie a string around your finger today to remind you not to lie. See how many times you catch yourself re-arranging the truth. Now, see how difficult it is to always talk the straight and narrow with your words.

tip

Store your outboard motor in the down position to prevent your lower unit from freezing.

DECEMBER 29

2 CORINTHIANS 5:17

If anyone belongs to Christ, there is a new creation.
The old things have gone; everything is made new!

WINTERTIME IS DOWNRIGHT DREARY. The coldness, dampness, and even grayness just seem to hang in the air. The longer the winter, the more we yearn for God to re–create our environment. We long for the dead–looking trees to turn green, the brown grass to disappear, the flowers to bloom, the gardens to be tempting with delicious vegetables. We long for the signs of new life. God warms the water and rejuvenates the fishing. Winter and springtime are pictures both of our lives and of what Jesus can do with us.

He takes the cold, dark parts of our life in sin and turns us into the bright, smiling, loving, and forgiving new creations of His righteousness He intended us to be.

✝ip

Never overlook
a single stick–up
or stump in
open water flats.

NEHEMIAH 9:20

"You gave your good Spirit to teach them."

LEARNING TO FISH is a never–ending challenge.
I know how to catch fish, yet I learn more every
time I go. We cannot attain perfection in fishing.

So it is with our daily walk with Christ.
We're saved, but not yet perfect. We will never
know all the answers, but God has given each of us
His Spirit to guide us through this life journey.
Think of it: God's Spirit has the answers. Just like
with fishing advice, though, we can choose whether
or not to follow these instructions. Pay close
attention to the Spirit's lessons for you today.
You have in you the very best personal
instructor to help you become the very
best person you can be.

Tip

Light will penetrate
the water about
twice the depth at
you can see a
white spinnerbait.

REVELATION 22:21

The grace of the Lord Jesus be with all.

THE LAST DAY OF THE YEAR to me is as exciting
as the first as we look back upon what we have
been through and look forward to what is to come.
The two are separated by 365 days, yet forever tied
together by the simple stroke of the clock.

Many times, we are so close yet still so far
away from Christ. Jesus has offered and paid for a
relationship that will never end. His direction and
His purpose from God the Father was to establish
that relationship with you and me. How very
special we must be to God. How important our
salvation must be to Him. If you are saved, never
take it for granted. If you are not
saved, find someone today and ask
them how you can be saved. May the
grace of my Lord Jesus be with
you forever.

† ι ρ

Take someone fishing;
enjoy God's
great outdoors;
and share the love of
Jesus with a friend.

To Learn More

JIMMY HOUSTON, "America's Favorite Fisherman," is a two-time Bass Angler Sportsman Society (BASS) Angler of the Year, has won ten national tournaments and has placed among the top money winners in more than one hundred national fishing events. He is also the author of *Hooked for Life* and *The Reel Line*.

The Fellowship Of Christian Anglers Society (FOCAS) was founded in 1983 by a handful of Christian fishermen who desired to worship and serve as disciples of Christ. Among this group were Jimmy Houston, Chris Houston, Hank Parker, Homer Circle, Al Lindner, Ray Scott, and others. They wanted the ministry to serve as a bond between all fishermen and to make sportfishermen into ". . . fishers of men" (Matthew 4:19).

For more information about FOCAS, please visit www.focas.org.